AD
A SHOPPER'S
GUIDE

A Supermarket Guide to Popular
Processed Foods

Jennifer Pulling

CENTURY
London Melbourne Auckland Johannesburg

To Duncan,
in gratitude for the hours
spent tearing round supermarkets
with me

First published in 1985 by Century Hutchinson Ltd,
Brookmount House, 62–65 Chandos Place, Covent Garden,
London WC2N 4NW
Century Hutchinson Publishing Group (Australia) Pty Ltd,
16–22 Church Street, Hawthorn, Melbourne, Victoria 3122
Century Hutchinson Group (NZ) Ltd,
32–34 View Road, PO Box 40–086, Glenfield, Auckland 10
Century Hutchinson Group (SA) Pty Ltd,
PO Box 337, Bergvlei 2012, South Africa

British Library Cataloguing in Publication Data
Pulling, Jenny
   Additives : a shoppers guide : a product-by-product
   guide to food labels.
   1. Food additives
   I. Title
   664'.06   TX553.A3

ISBN 0 7126 9480 3

Printed in Great Britain by Photobooks (Bristol) Ltd, Bristol, Avon

Contents

Foreword

by Dr Peter Mansfield M.A., M.B., B.Chir. (Cantab.)

Artificial additives in food are a major issue for the modern housewife. Most of their names are Greek to her. They were devised for the convenience of processed food manufacturers, and sanctioned by government agencies largely dependent on information supplied by them. The practical interests of the housewife and mother were not considered. And if she asks how safe they are, science cannot tell her. We have all unwittingly been made guinea pigs in a gigantic human toxicity trial. We shall know the results soon enough.

But information is at last becoming available, and will be required by law after January 1986. What we are told only makes clear how little we are allowed to know. Complex irritant chemicals are lined up alongside innocent nutrients in a number code—the E code—which conceals more than it reveals. However is the shopping public to make head or tail of it?

Jennifer Pulling has blazed the trail for you. By examining large numbers of familiar products and explaining their labels, she begins the process of your enlightenment.

Your discoveries will prompt in you further questions she cannot answer. Do not blame her for that. She has made the best of what little we are told. Go instead to doctors, MPs and public health inspectors seeking answers. They will have to probe in turn.

Little by little we will have the truth, reluctantly let out in dribs and drabs by public bodies under pressure. Then at last we may get sanity to override convenience in food technology.

We all have a lot to gain.

IMPORTANT NOTE

Whilst the additives shown in the following pages were those appearing on the various products at the time this book was researched, it must be appreciated that they amount in volume to a very small proportion of the whole contents. The inclusion of a particular additive or additives does not indicate that the consumer will be adversely affected by the normal consumption of any particular product. The examples given are intended as a guide to what may occur if certain substances are taken in excess and to the fact that some people, e.g. asthmatics, may be more susceptible to particular additives than others.

Author's Note on
Sugar and Salt Ratings

Throughout the guide, products have been awarded a certain number of stars.

I have given one star to those products whose sugar and salt content is low; two stars for a fairly high content of sugar and salt and three for those whose content is really high in sugar or salt additives. Occasionally I have given a three star plus where items contain a considerable amount of sugar as well as artificial sweeteners.

This rating is based on several criteria: their position on the label has usually dictated my scorings; I have also awarded extra stars where artificial sweeteners appeared in the list of ingredients. A third consideration and one that I am inclined to study, I believe in common with many shoppers, is the relationship of one brand to another within a certain category.

Brand Ratings

The brands and 'own brand' names mentioned throughout the guide have been graded into those which contain less additives ranging down to those that contain more. This has been my choice but there will be occasions when the shopper may choose to put one brand before another in preference where certain health problems dictate which additives he or she must individually avoid. Please see the Important Note on page v.

As I have said before, this book is to guide you through the lists of 'E' additives. Everybody is an individual with individual considerations. These include those of health, personal taste and, important these days, the question of the cost of living. The final choice is up to you.

Introduction

This book is not meant to scare you away from the supermarket and its often tempting array of tins, packets, bottles and boxes. In a perfect world, with time at our disposal, these would not be necessary; we would prepare all our food freshly, from ingredients grown in our gardens, from free range meat and eggs, and whole, unrefined grains. We would set our tables attractively and relax to enjoy our meals. But life today will not slow down or become more simple, nor is it possible to opt out of all its demands on us. Whether we approve of them or not, convenience, fast, 'instant' foods are here to stay and, used with discretion, can be a boon to the busy housewife and worker. Our society, for better or for worse, has become one of the 'television snack' and confectionery bars to nibble and chew while on the move.

But this is not the place to try to tell you what you should or should not be eating—although there is much to recommend a diet that relies largely on fresh, whole foods and does not resort too often to the tin opener. Every family has its favourites, however, and the outcry can be imagined if they were suddenly cut right out of the menu, even if they are not all necessarily 'good' for us.

We start from the point then that it is very difficult to avoid additives altogether. So much of our food is laced with them: emulsifiers, preservatives, anti-oxidants and flavourings, it is no small wonder they are becoming of major concern among shoppers foxed by the ubiquitous 'E' numbers. The good news is that their obligatory inclusion in the list of ingredients can help us to have more control over precisely what we are eating, if we know what they mean and how negatively they appear on the labels of our favourite products.

The intention of this book, therefore—for which the

research was carried out between August and mid-September 1985—is to guide you through that growing, often bewildering maze of substances so that at least you will know which additives are dangerous or suspect in the foods you regularly buy and eat, which are supposed to be safe, and thus you can make your decision as to what you will avoid.

Suppose, for example, baked beans or strawberry jam feature on your shopping list. With this guide in hand, you can see at a glance which brand contains flavourings and which does not, whether a brand is high in sugar or whether it is low—from then on it is up to you.

Our concern as shoppers has become that of some of the major retailers and manufacturers. Some of them have announced that they are trying to remove those additives which are most seriously suspect, when they can. In the following pages, you will find several products for which there has been an earnest attempt to keep them as additive free as possible. This is a positive sign and, it is to be hoped, an example that will be followed. On the other hand, there are products listed in which the manufacturer has used additives simply for convenience sake, allowing him to disguise the lack of natural ingredients in food, or in order to make a product look as if it is nourishing and attractive when, in fact, there is little or no nutritional value.

'Additive' has become a somewhat dirty word but not all additives are synthetic or bad for us. As an example, E300, which is more commonly known as vitamin C, is used to stop fruits browning or fats going rancid, and certainly improves the quality of such foods. Other antioxidants, such as E320 butylated hydroxyanisole, have a more dubious record of safety.

If there were no antioxidants used, you would not be able to buy many of the packeted goods from a supermarket shelf—their life would be impractically short and they would cost a good deal more. But in the case of many of them, it is the manufacturer who benefits and not you, the consumer.

Preservatives which inhibit the growth of micro-organisms can include natural acids such as 296 malic acid or E260 acetic acid but they may also be sulphites like E223 sodium metabisulphite which are dangerous to asthmatics, or nitrates E251 which break down into nitrites (E249, E250) in the body. These may interact with amines from foods in the stomach to form nitrosamines, a known cause of cancer in animals.

Many of the emulsifiers and stabilisers have natural origins and are safe, such as lecithin E322 which is actually used therapeutically to mobilise fats in the body. On the other hand, the polyphosphates E450(b) and E450(c) have been indicted with causing digestive disturbances because they can block a number of enzymes.

Flavourings are not subject to government control, and are a feature of many products. The 'Flavour enhancer' 621 monosodium glutamate is responsible for a number of allergic reactions. It is also taboo in or on foods intended specifically for babies and young children.

Two other flavour enhancers, 631 sodium inosinate and 627 guanosine 5, are also not permitted in foods intended for little children and yet they both appear in the list of ingredients of gravy granules which is surely an item consumed by *all* the family!

Fats and soaps such as E470 and E471 are used in products like cake and dessert mixes to replace natural but perishable ingredients and thereby increase their shelf life. They may not be harmful but they lead the consumer to think that he or she is buying a much more nutritious item than is really the case. The same thing goes for other additives used to swell food with water, air or other kinds of volume which has no nutritional value. These include the gums like E412 guar gum, celluloses E466 carboxymethyl-cellulose, gelling agents and the polyphosphates.

Colourings which are used to make a product look more attractive are frequently synthetic 'coal tar' and azo-dyes. These provoke allergic reactions in an appreciable minority of people. One big problem is that they are a feature of many foods that are children's favourites—fish fingers, dessert whips, sweets and jellies. Another instance is the blackcurrant so-called 'health' drink. Products in this guide include E123 amaranth, E102 tartrazine and E142 acid brilliant green in the lists of ingredients. Because of the cancer-forming quality and damage to liver and sex organs which was shown in animal studies, countries including the USA and Russia have banned amaranth. In a recent study at the Great Ormond Street Hospital for Sick Children, tartrazine was shown to provoke hypersensitivity in four out of five children tested, as did the benzoates E210–E219. Acid brilliant green appears on a list drawn up by the then Food Additives and Contaminants Committee, in 1979. This 'B' list comprised additives which were to be regarded as provisionally accepted but which, in some cases, caused sufficient disquiet to demand new toxicological tests, to be completed within two years. While such tests continue, so does the situation whereby one or more additives to a product may be withdrawn after being banned as unsafe, while others equally likely to cause allergic reactions continue in use.

It is not only children who suffer. Acute reactions by susceptible adults which include skin rashes, swellings, purple patches on the skin, blurred vision and problems with breathing are reported; these are particularly common among those who are aspirin sensitive, asthmatic, or prone to allergies. The azo-dyes which are found in many commonly used items such as margarine, biscuits, cheese and orange squash make life difficult for anyone with such tendencies.

At least if you do suffer a pronounced adverse reaction to an additive you have warning and can set about excluding it from your diet. Long-term consumption with no apparent or immediate bad effects could well be piling up problems for the future. As cancer prevention advice expert Dr Jan de Winter has pointed out: it is long-term habit and faulty nutrition over a period of years which are the problems. Degenerative diseases which are on the increase in our Western society do not develop overnight but are the accumulative result of poor life-style and eating habits. And while individual research on isolated additives is carried out on animals, no one has yet researched the combined effects of the quantity of additives used in our food, or carried out that research on human beings.

Dr de Winter, like many doctors, also indicts sugar and salt as substances that can seriously damage our health. He advises that we should cut down if not eliminate the quantities we take in our diet. Half an hour in a supermarket will confirm that it is not very difficult to eat the national average of a kilo of sugar a week, even though most people confronted by that figure would deny they ate anything like it. But it is true, for the vast majority of shoppers: human beings have a sweet tooth. Our language is filled with expressions implying that something sweet is 'nice'. Sugar has long been used to mask unpleasant flavours, or make food more palatable, but it is only comparatively recently that it has invaded our lives in such an enormous avalanche.

While other changes in our diet have happened over many hundreds of years, it is only within the last century that we have eaten such enormous quantities of refined sugar. If, for example, you eat a medium slice of chocolate cake, you could be taking into your body the equivalent of 12 teaspoonfuls of sugar; a bottle of cola will give you the equivalent of 4 teaspoonfuls, the same amount in a small doughnut. Because of our consumption of this 'hidden sugar' we in the UK are now eating 25 times the amount of sugar we ate a hundred years ago.

A problem that crops up is that, in this concentrated form, we can eat amounts far greater than we could in its natural form. Such sugar satisfies our appetites but offers no nutrients. It simply presents our bodies with a substance they cannot use. If we lived in a more natural environment we would obtain sugar from unrefined cereals and fruits, and our normal capacity would not allow us to eat more than a certain amount.

It is true, of course, that the brain and nervous system need glucose to function and this has confused many people. They believe that glucose is necessary —our source of energy—that it helps us 'work, rest and play' and the

advertiser homes in on that belief. Mothers are nudged
into believing that they are failing their children if they do
not give them the chocolate bars that will 'keep them
going' until the next meal. We see miraculous recovery by
invalids who are fed glucose drinks, and runners just keep
on running after a glucose tablet or two. It is as well,
therefore, to define more clearly the words 'sugar' and
'glucose'. We need glucose as an essential fuel for the body,
particularly for the nervous system, but we do not need to
eat glucose. It should enter our bodies as part of unrefined
and complex foods which are broken down gradually, step
by step, until they pass into the blood as glucose. That
which is not immediately needed is stored in the liver as
glycogen, a reserve supply, and the rest is utilised for
energy. If you eat huge amounts of sugar, in its various
refined forms, the normal digestive processes cannot cope
and the body is strained severely by the tidal wave of
glucose that results.

There are several different kinds of sugar, though the
most familiar by far is the sucrose we buy in packets, from
which we get that 'spoonful of sugar' which helps the
medicine go down, not to mention sweetening a cup of tea.

Single Sugars (Mono-saccharides)

Fructose   This is the oldest sweetener known to man which
has always featured in his food system since it is found, in
the free form, in almost all sweet fruits and berries.
Glucose   The most widely distributed sugar in nature:
found in the blood, oxidised in the cells to furnish energy,
and stored in the liver as glycogen. The processes used in
the glucose syrup industry are modelled on our natural
conversion of starch—through dextrins and sugars—to
dextrose (glucose or blood sugar).
Galactose   This is obtained from lactose (milk sugar) and
not found free in nature.

Double Sugars (Di-saccharides)

Sucrose Obtained from sugar cane and sugar beet. This cannot be directly absorbed by our bloodstream but must first be split into two single sugars, glucose and fructose, by enzymes in the small intestine, which are then absorbed individually or converted to glycogen.

Maltose (malt sugar) Found in barley and honey though it is chiefly produced from starch broken down by the saliva and pancreatic secretions. This must be split by enzymes in the small intestine into glucose before it can be used.

Lactose (milk sugar) This is like the other double sugars and cannot be used by the body until it is broken down by the digestive enzymes into two single sugars, glucose and galactose.

Multi-Sugars (Poly-saccharides)

These include the starches, cellulose and glycogen. They are made up of glucose units joined together and cannot be used by our bodies until separated by digestive processes.

There are many other less important sugars but all can be recognised on food labels because they end in 'ose' and usually they end up in our bloodstream as glucose. Many vegetables and all cereals contain starches which are split up into glucose. There is, therefore, no danger of going short of glucose to the brain.

We created problems for ourselves when we discovered we could refine and concentrate natural sugar. In its natural state, sugar cane contains all the vitamins and minerals we need to use it properly. But when it is refined these nutrients are removed leaving 100 per cent sucrose. They are discarded as molasses, which is actually more nourishing than the sugar. It contains useful amounts of iron, calcium, zinc, copper and chromium which are needed to process the sugar in our bodies. In effect, refinement makes sugar an anti-nutrient.

Sucrose as a highly refined food provides 'dead calories', about 500 a day in the typical British diet, which may replace more nutritious foods or be eaten additionally. It figures largely in a concern of many shoppers about their food: they want to control their food intake in order to avoid obesity and they do not like interference with their food. Sucrose is guilty on both counts.

Professor John Yudkin, in his book *Pure, White and Deadly*, made a chilling statement: 'If only a small fraction of what is already known about the facts of sugar were to be revealed in relation to any other material used as a food additive the material would be promptly banned.'

During this century there has been an 80 per cent increase in coronary deaths in the UK. Changes in our diet and particularly the intake of more and more refined sugar are contributing to this incidence of degenerative diseases.

Too much sugar in the diet can also affect behaviour. Studies in America, reinforced by British research, have revealed that foods high in sugars and refined starches, and deficient in nutrients, may affect not only our bodies but our minds. The director of the American New Life Foundation Trust, the Reverend Vic Ramsey, weaned young drug addicts off their diet of foods high in refined sugars and starches, junk and convenience foods, and fed them whole foods. He noticed marked changes in the youngsters' behaviour patterns, including less aggression and violence.

In his book *Feed Your Kids Right*, Dr Lendon Smith underlined refined starches as a cause of misbehaviour among children. He suggested that the increased amount of hyperactivity and problems suspected to be psycho-logical were, in fact, related to a high intake of sugar. It is something that preoccupies Sally Bunday, founder of the Hyperactive Children's Support Group, and according to Peter Hudson, homoeopath and nutritionist: 'Sucrose places the body in a permanent state of stress in which repair is impossible. Sugar, white, brown or in whatever form, is one of the most ageing ingredients we can take into our stomachs.'

In his book *Why Die Young?*, Hudson suggests that if you want to give up sugar you should avoid manufactured biscuits, cakes, sweets, puddings and breakfast cereals. Choose porridge oats, muesli or other goods advertised as made from wholegrains. Avoid artificial or refined sweeteners.

While children are tiny it is relatively easy to teach them to shun 'neat' sugar and give them a crunchy celery stick or piece of apple instead of chocolate. But, as writer and child expert Penelope Leach has pointed out, it is foolish to try to ban all sweets from a child's diet. Rather than create a forbidden fruit that will become more desirable, to be eaten secretly, it is better to allow children a ration which they eat at a set time. Afterwards they should clean their teeth.

It is hard to avoid all sugar but we can become more aware. We can examine the labels on the packet or tin of our favourite foods. We can control the amount of 'hidden sugar' which enters our bodies.

How Sugar is Used in Some of Our Foods

Sucrose   As well as giving sweetness to foods sucrose is used as a filler, diluent and sometimes to 'carry' such ingredients as flavours and colours. Its ability to bind water and so make it unavailable to support organisms that might spoil the product, makes it useful as a preservative. As an example, the addition of sucrose in fruit processing such as jam making has become both necessary and customary— few fruits contain sufficient sugar to ensure their flavour and texture preservation alone. For canned fruits, sucrose is used to preserve the texture and general appearance of fruits, keeping oxidation to the minimum.

At levels up to 2 per cent it improves the flavours of sauces, soups, mayonnaise, cheese and yoghurt, among others. The taste of sausages is improved by adding 1 per cent sugar and it also helps to stabilise meat's red colour which is sought after by shoppers.

Glucose Syrups   These are used in the making of bread, buns and cakes. They help to retain moisture, and to prevent staleness and drying out under varying conditions. This is particularly important in the keeping qualities of sponge-type cakes.

They help to give gloss and body to fruit pie fillings.

Different kinds of ice cream contain glucose syrups which function in several ways: they stop too much crystallisation, give a better freezing point control, contribute to the body of the product and its feel in the mouth, and give a balanced sweetness.

Glucose syrups are also useful in soft drinks which contain saccharin as the two seem to balance each other in terms of sweetness without bitter after-taste.

Malt Syrups   These were, at first, concentrates of the water soluble extract of malt. Recently, the term 'malt syrups' has been misused to suggest that they are also those produced from starch where at least one-third of the sugar content is maltose. These kinds of syrups are more correctly called maltose syrups.

Malt syrups are not just providers of sweetness and calories but they also give flavour, natural colour and essential amino acids and vitamins.

Maltose syrups are currently used in frozen desserts to control the formation of crystals.

Dextrose   It is used as a sweetener, an aid to browning and to lengthen shelf life in such products as biscuits and cakes. It is also used to 'dust' swiss rolls and doughnuts.

Dextrose is used quite substantially in tinned and packeted goods such as soups, gravies, sauces and citrus juices; in dry mixes as a 'carrier' for instant drinks, flavours and spices; in pickles—dependent on the variety, making up from 25 per cent to 35 per cent of the pickling juices; and in a wide variety of meat products such as chopped ham and luncheon meats.

High Fructose Glucose Syrup   Ice cream manufacturers have found it a valuable addition to their range of sweeteners.

Dairy manufacturers use it in chocolate milk and it is incorporated with other glucose syrups in frozen desserts.

Tomato ketchup made with high fructose glucose syrup will keep a deep red colour and has a 'clean' sweetness.

It is replacing a large portion of sucrose in many jams, jellies and preserves.

Lactose   It is used in such items as custard, fruit pies, hams and preserves to give an extra thickness and pleasant 'mouth feel'. In baked goods it gives better flavour and texture, and enhances shelf life and toasting properties.

Lactose can stabilise proteins and has been used to prepare certain whipped dessert products.

The first hydrogenated sugar to be manufactured was sorbitol in the 1930s. It is now used in food manufacture as a sweetening agent and also stabilises a product and helps to prevent it drying out. If it is added to sucrose-containing syrups it reduces the tendency to form crystals.

This was followed by mannitol which is used to add texture, to help prevent products drying out, as a sweetener in products which are sugar-free and to prevent particles sticking together.

After these came hydrogenated glucose syrups and finally xylitol. These all appear on the list of permitted sweeteners although only sorbitol and mannitol have 'E' numbers. Some forms of saccharin, and isomalt, are also listed as permitted sweeteners.

In the case of saccharin, studies have seemed to clear it of blame but it is important to remember that certain people are more sensitive to synthetic substances than others. A safe policy is to limit the amount of the substance you use as much as possible. Regulations concerning the introduction of new artificial sweeteners are strict in the UK so that acesulfame, potassium, aspartame, thaumatin together with xylitol were exhaustively tested before the revision of regulations in 1983 allowed them to be added.

Salt

Our bodies need dietary salt (sodium chloride) but they need it in correct balance to potassium. At one time, before salt became so popular and was not used as generously to flavour and conserve foods, our diets were higher in potassium and lower in sodium. Now the position seems to be completely reversed and many of us have not adapted well to that change in ratio. According to recent information, it seems that about 20 per cent of the population has a predisposition to hypertension and may be sensitive to salt which is the mineral in our diets most generally suspected of encouraging it.

Salt is not a bad thing in itself but is easily over-consumed. This stresses our adrenals, kidneys and heart and is considered a factor in the accumulation of mineralised deposits in the joints which can result in rheumatoid arthritis. Salt retention is a factor in water retention and cellulite.

Salt can also become addictive and these days many of us seem to use it as if it were a drug. Not only do we add it to the cooking water, to sauces and stews, but we sprinkle it liberally over food at table, often without tasting it first. But sodium is of such importance to the body that it figures in practically all foods we eat. There is really no necessity to add salt.

Check this yourself. If you find it difficult to give up using salt in your food, you are probably mildly addicted. In one study, people who suffered from hypertension chose more salt in their diets than others who did not have the problem; they were effectively hooked on a substance that was causing them harm.

According to Peter Hudson, a principal cause of an over-acid bloodstream is the taking of too much salt. 'An unsalted body is a younger one, a more relaxed body', he writes. 'It is a myth that we need to eat salt, for fruits and vegetables in our diet provide us with as much as we need.'

Our children may become salt addicted without our realising it. Earl Mindel, author of the *Vitamin Bible*, points out that a teenage boy who eats a fast food burger will certainly receive 44 per cent of his requirements for protein, but also 963mg of sodium. Potatoes are a good source of vitamins and minerals and even if you bend to your child's demands and give them to him fried, 9oz will provide only 8mg of sodium. Let him or her buy just 5½oz of chips at a fast food place and they will consume 117mg of sodium.

Salt is one of the most popular preservatives for food but we need to control how much of it we allow to enter our bodies. Current recommendations for a good healthy diet include limiting the amount of sodium we eat. This means we should decrease consumption of foods with a lot of 'hidden salt' which include smoked and cured meats, snack foods, canned vegetables and other processed foods where salt is high on the list of ingredients or where salt is added directly to food.

Gradually, your sense of taste will develop and soon the addition of salt to food appears unnecessary.

Apple Pies

MR KIPLING BRAMLEY APPLE PIES

Sugar***   *Salt**

Modified Starch Used as thickener. An umbrella term for 18 substances not defined by 'E' numbers.
Effects on Health No suggestion that they are harmful.

'Emulsifier' One of a large group of permitted substances, which will have to be specified on the label after 1 January 1986.
Effects on Health From the little information available, it does not appear that serious health hazard is incurred with these.

'Preservative' possibly **E202 Potassium Sorbate**
Effects on Health No health risk known.
or
296 Malic Acid
Effects on Health No health risk known.

SAINSBURY'S APPLE PIE

Sugar***   *Salt**

Modified Starch Used as thickener. An umbrella term for 18 substances not defined by 'E' numbers.
Effects on Health No suggestion that they are harmful.

E330 Citric Acid Stabilises the acidity of food substances, prevents discoloration of fruit, keeps the flavour 'true' and retains vitamin C.
Effects on Health Needs to be taken in very large quantities to erode teeth or cause local irritation.

296 Malic Acid Used to flavour, an acid derived from apples.
Effects on Health No health risks known.

E202 Potassium Sorbate A preservative that is antifungal and antibacterial.
Effects on Health No known health risk.

also

SAFEWAY APPLE PIE

WAITROSE APPLE PIE
Sugar ***   *Salt**

Modified Starch Used as thickener. An umbrella term for 18 substances not defined by 'E' numbers.
Effects on Health No suggestion that they are harmful.

E450(a) Tetrasodium Diphosphate Maintains acidity/alkalinity at determined level, an emulsifying salt and stabiliser, also gelling agent.
Effects on Health No health risks known.

500 Sodium Bicarbonate Used to balance alkaline/acidity levels and to aerate.
Effects on Health Not known as a health risk.

E330 Citric Acid Stabilises the acidity of food substances, prevents discoloration of fruit, keeps the flavour 'true' and retains vitamin C.
Effects on Health Needs to be taken in very large quantities to erode teeth or cause local irritation.

296 Malic Acid Used to flavour, an acid derived from apples.
Effects on Health No health risks known.

E202 Potassium Sorbate A preservative that is antifungal and antibacterial.
Effects on Health No known health risks.

LEON'S APPLE PIE
Sugar *** plus   *Salt**

E420(11) Sorbitol Syrup Used for sweetening and also to prevent products from drying out.
Effects on Health When taken to excess it can cause flatulence and distension of stomach. It is, however, of use to diabetics as it does not raise the blood sugar level significantly and is well tolerated.

E330 Citric Acid Stabilises the acidity of food substances, prevents discoloration of fruit, keeps the flavour 'true' and retains vitamin C.
Effects on Health Needs to be taken in very large quantities to erode teeth or cause local irritation.

E202 Potassium Sorbate A preservative that is antifungal and antibacterial.
Effects on Health Not known as a health risk.

Flavourings
Effects on Health Debatable, as no information is available. Many substances in this category are artificially synthesised; safety cannot be assumed.

Baked Beans

WAITROSE
(*All Natural Ingredients Brand*)

E412 Guar Gum Thickener or dietary bulker.
Effects on Health Harmless except in excess when stomach cramps, nausea and flatulence might result.

HEINZ
*Sugar*** *Salt***

Modified Starch Used as thickener. An umbrella term for 18 substances not defined by 'E' numbers.
Effects on Health No suggestion that they are harmful.

CO-OP
*Sugar*** *Salt***

Modified Starch Used as thickener. An umbrella term for 18 substances not defined by 'E' numbers.
Effects on Health No suggestion that they are harmful.

500 Sodium Bicarbonate Used as a base, to increase alkalinity or reduce acidity.
Effects on Health Does not cause any known harm.

HP
*Sugar*** *Salt***

Modified Starch Used as thickener. An umbrella term for 18 substances not defined by 'E' numbers.
Effects on Health No suggestion that they are harmful.

Flavourings
Effects on Health Debatable, as no information is available. Many substances in this category are artificially synthesised; safety cannot be assumed.

Beefburgers from the Frozen Cabinet

DALEPAK BEEF DALESTEAKS
Sugar   Salt**

Flavourings
Effects on Health Debatable, as no information is available. Many substances in this category are artificially synthesised; safety cannot be assumed.

TIFFANYS BEEFBURGERS
Sugar**   Salt**

Flavourings
Effects on Health Debatable, as no information is available. Many substances in this category are artificially synthesised; safety cannot be assumed.

E450(a) Tetrasodium Diphosphate Maintains
acidity/alkalinity at determined level, an emulsifying salt and stabiliser, also gelling agent.
Effects on Health No health risks known.

also

SAFEWAY BEEFBURGERS

TESCO BEEFBURGERS
Sugar   Salt**

E450(c) Sodium Polyphosphates
Emulsifying salt used to stabilise.
Effects on Health There is a suggestion that polyphosphates can block a number of enzymes causing digestive disturbances.

554 Calcium Polyphosphates
An emulsifying salt.
Effects on Health There is a suggestion that polyphosphates can block a number of enzymes causing digestive disturbances.

621 Monosodium Glutamate
Enhances the flavour of foods containing protein by stimulating the taste buds or increasing the degree of saliva produced in the mouth.
Effects on Health Responsible for symptoms of palpitation, headache, dizziness, muscle tightness, nausea, feeling of weakness in the forearms, pains in the neck, and other, migraine-like symptoms in some people. This substance is recommended to be excluded from the diets of hyperactive

children; it is also taboo in or on food intended for babies and young children.

BIRD'S EYE STEAKHOUSE
Sugar   *Salt***

Flavourings
Effects on Health Debatable, as no information is available. Many substances in this category are artificially synthesised; safety cannot be assumed.

'Polyphosphates' possibly E450(c) Sodium Polyphosphates or 544 Calcium Polyphosphates
Effects on Health There is a suggestion that polyphosphates can block a number of enzymes causing digestive disturbances.

621 Monosodium Glutamate
Enhances the flavour of foods containing protein by stimulating the taste buds or increasing the degree of saliva produced in the mouth.
Effects on Health Responsible for symptoms of palpitation, headache, dizziness, muscle tightness, nausea, feeling of weakness in the forearms, pains in the neck, and other, migraine-like symptoms in some people. This substance is recommended to be excluded from the diets of hyperactive children; it is also taboo in or on food intended for babies and young children.

E223 Sodium Metabisulphite
Used to preserve, an antioxidant.
Effects on Health A member of the sulphite family which is harmful to asthmatics and may cause gastric irritation by releasing sulphurous acid. Can cause allergies and aversions.

Blackcurrant Health Drink

RIBENA
Sugar***   *Salt*

No artificial colouring, flavouring, or sweetener

E211 Sodium Benzoate
Preserves; is antibacterial and antifungal.

Effects on Health People who are prone to skin rashes or are asthmatic may react with allergic symptoms. This additive is one that is recommended by the Hyperactive Children's Support Group to be avoided by food-sensitive children and adults who are aspirin sensitive.

E223 Sodium Metabisulphite
Used as an antioxidant and to
preserve.
Effects on Health A member of
the sulphite family which is
harmful to asthmatics and may
cause gastric irritation by
releasing sulphurous acid. Can
cause allergies and aversions.

SAINSBURY'S BLACKCURRANT HEALTH DRINK

Sugar***   *Salt*

E330 Citric Acid Stabilises the
acidity of fruit substances,
prevents the discoloration of
fruit, keeps the flavour 'true'
and retains vitamin C.
Effects on Health Needs to be
consumed in very large
quantities to erode teeth or
irritate locally.

E211 Sodium Benzoate
Preserves; is antibacterial and
antifungal.
Effects on Health People who are
prone to skin rashes or are
asthmatic may react with
allergic symptoms. This additive
is one that is recommended by
the Hyperactive Children's
Support Group to be avoided
by food-sensitive children and
adults who are aspirin sensitive.

E223 Sodium Metabisulphite
Used as an antioxidant and to
preserve
Effects on Health A member of
the sulphite family which is

harmful to asthmatics and may
cause gastric irritation by
releasing sulphurous acid. Can
cause allergies and aversions.

E123 Amaranth Gives red
colouring to product.
Effects on Health As an azo-dye it
should be avoided by people
who are sensitive to aspirin as it
may cause a skin rash. The
Hyperactive Children's Support
Group recommend it is
excluded from the diets of food-
sensitive children.

E142 Acid Brilliant Green
Gives green colouring to
product.
Effects on Health No ill effects
reported although, as an azo-
dye, it may affect hyperactive
children and those who suffer
from asthma or are aspirin
sensitive.

E102 Tartrazine Gives yellow
colouring to product.
Effects on Health Has been
implicated as causing
sleeplessness at night in
hyperactive and food-sensitive
children. Symptoms including
skin rashes, hay fever, problems
with breathing, blurred vision
and purple skin patches are
reported in susceptible people,
particularly those who are
aspirin sensitive.

also

TESCO BLACKCURRANT CONCENTRATED HEALTH DRINK

Flavourings
Effects on Health Debatable, as
no information is available.
Many substances in this
category are artificially
synthesised; safety cannot be
assumed.

CO-OP
BLACKCURRANT
HEALTH DRINK
Sugar***   *Salt*

E330 Citric Acid Stabilises the
acidity of food substances,
prevents discoloration of fruit,
keeps the flavour 'true' and
retains vitamin C.
Effects on Health Needs to be
consumed in very large
quantities to erode teeth or
irritate locally.

E150 Caramel Gives brown
colouring to product and is used
as a flavouring.
Effects on Health A question
mark as to its safety hangs over
this additive. There has been a
reduction in the number of
kinds available to the food
industry. Work is in hand to
discover the safest form. One
kind is produced with ammonia
and has been shown to cause
vitamin B6 deficiency in rats.

E123 Amaranth Gives red
colouring to product.
Effects on Health As an azo-dye it
should be avoided by people
who are sensitive to aspirin as it

may cause a skin rash. The
Hyperactive Children's Support
Group recommend it is
excluded from the diets of food-
sensitive children.

E142 Acid Brilliant Green
Gives green colouring to
product.
Effects on Health No ill effects
reported although, as an azo-
dye, it may affect hyperactive
children and those who suffer
from asthma or are aspirin
sensitive.

E211 Sodium Benzoate
Preserves; is antibacterial and
antifungal.
Effects on Health People who are
prone to skin rashes or are
asthmatic may react with
allergic symptoms. This additive
is one that is recommended by
the Hyperactive Children's
Support Group to be avoided
by food-sensitive children and
adults who are aspirin sensitive.

E223 Sodium Metabisulphite
Used as an antioxidant and to
preserve.
Effects on Health A member of
the sulphite family which is
harmful to asthmatics and may
cause gastric irritation by
releasing sulphurous acid. Can
cause allergies and aversions.

Flavourings
Effects on Health Debatable, as
no information is available.
Many substances in this
category are artificially
synthesised; safety cannot be
assumed.

See Note p. v

Bread Rolls

MOTHER'S PRIDE CRUSTY BREAKFAST ROLLS

Sugar***   *Salt***

E472(e) Mono- and Diacetyltartaric Acid Esters of Mono- and Di-glycerides of Fatty Acids Used to emulsify or stabilise.
Effects on Health There are no known health risks.

VITBE WHEATGERM SNACK ROLLS

Sugar**   *Salt***

E472(e) Mono- and Diacetyltartaric Acid Esters of Mono- and Di-glycerides of Fatty Acids Used to emulsify or stabilise.
Effects on Health There are no known health risks.

E282 Calcium Propionate
Used to preserve and to inhibit moulds, particularly two which are heat resistant.
Effects on Health There are no health risks.

also

FINE FARE SOFT BAKE LUNCH ROLLS

SAINSBURY'S MORNING ROLLS

Sugar**   *Salt***

E471 Mono- and Di-glycerides of Fatty Acids Used to emulsify and stabilise.
Effects on Health Not known as a health risk.

E472(e) Mono- and Diacetyltartaric Acid Esters of Mono- and Di-glycerides of Fatty Acids Used to emulsify or stabilise.
Effects on Health There are no known health risks.

E481 Sodium Stearoyl-2-Lactylate Used to stabilise and emulsify.
Effects on Health Not known as a health risk.

E282 Calcium Propionate
Used to preserve and to inhibit moulds, particularly two which are heat resistant.
Effects on Health There are no health risks.

Brown Sauce

SAINSBURY'S BROWN SAUCE

Sugar **   *Salt* **

Modified Starch Used as thickener. An umbrella term for 18 substances not defined by 'E' numbers.
Effects on Health No suggestion that they are harmful.

DADDIE'S SAUCE

Sugar **   *Salt* **

Modified Starch Used as thickener. An umbrella term for 18 substances not defined by 'E' numbers.
Effects on Health No suggestion that they are harmful.

E150 Caramel Gives brown colour to product and is used as a flavouring.
Effects on Health A question mark as to its safety hangs over this additive. There has been a reduction in the number of kinds available to the food industry. Work is in hand to discover the safest form. One kind which is produced with

ammonia has been shown to cause vitamin B6 deficiency in rats.

E202 Potassium Sorbate A preservative that is antifungal and antibacterial.
Effects on Health No health risks known.

TESCO BROWN SAUCE VALUE LTD

Sugar ***   *Salt* **

E260 Acetic Acid Antibacterial, used to stabilise acidity of food and dilute colouring matter.
Effects on Health No known ill effects.

E150 Caramel Gives brown colour to product and is used as a flavouring.
Effects on Health A question mark as to its safety hangs over this additive. There has been a reduction in the number of kinds available to the food industry. Work is in hand to discover the safest form. One kind which is produced with ammonia has been shown to

cause vitamin B6 deficiency in rats.

E412 Guar Gum Used to thicken; a bulking agent.
Effects on Health Harmless except when consumed to excess when nausea, flatulence and stomach cramps might occur.

E102 Tartrazine Gives yellow colour to product.
Effects on Health One of the azo-dye family which is recommended to be excluded from the diets of hyperactive children. Adults may have an allergic reaction with symptoms of skin rash, swollen blood vessels and gastric problems, especially if aspirin sensitive.

E122 Carmoisine Gives red colour to product.
Effects on Health This has been recommended by the Hyperactive Children's Support Group as unsuitable for children who are food sensitive. An azo-dye, it may produce adverse reactions in those people who have an aspirin allergy or are asthmatic. Such reactions can include skin rashes or swelling.

E151 Black PN Gives black colour to product.
Effects on Health Further research into the effects of this additive is needed. One 90-day feeding study on pigs revealed intestinal cysts. This features on the list of additives which the Hyperactive Children's Support Group do not recommend be given to hyperactive children.

SAFEWAY FRUITY SAUCE
Sugar***   *Salt***

E260 Acetic Acid
Antibacterial, used to stabilise acidity of food and dilute colouring matter.
Effects on Health No known ill effects.

E150 Caramel Gives brown colour to product and is used as a flavouring.
Effects on Health A question mark as to its safety hangs over this additive. There has been a reduction in the number of kinds available to the food industry. Work is in hand to discover the safest form. One kind which is produced with ammonia has been shown to cause vitamin B6 deficiency in rats.

E412 Guar Gum Used to thicken; a bulking agent.
Effects on Health Harmless except when consumed to excess, when nausea, flatulence and stomach cramps might occur.

E110 Sunset Yellow FCF
Gives yellow colour to product.
Effects on Health One of the azo-dye family which is recommended to be excluded from the diets of hyperactive children. Adults may have an allergic reaction with symptoms of skin rash, swollen blood vessels and gastric problems, especially if aspirin sensitive.

E124 Ponceau 4R Gives red colour to product.
Effects on Health One of the azo-dye family which is recommended to be excluded from the diets of hyperactive children. Adults who are aspirin sensitive or asthmatic may be affected.

E102 Tartrazine Gives yellow colour to product.
Effects on Health One of the azo-dye family which is recommended to be excluded from the diets of hyperactive children. Adults may have an allergic reaction with symptoms of skin rash, swollen blood vessels and gastric problems, especially if aspirin sensitive.

E122 Carmoisine Gives red colour to product.
Effects on Health This has been recommended by the Hyperactive Children's Support Group as unsuitable for children who are food sensitive. An azo-dye, it may produce adverse symptoms in those people who have an aspirin allergy or are asthmatic.

E151 Black PN Gives black colour to product.
Effects on Health Further research into the effects of this additive is needed. One 90-day feeding study on pigs revealed intestinal cysts. This features on the list of additives which the Hyperactive Children's Support Group do not recommend be given to hyperactive children.

Cheese Cake Mix

GREEN'S CHEESE CAKE MIX LUXURY RECIPE

Sugar***   *Salt*

E320 Butylated Hydroxyanisole As an antioxidant this works alone or in conjunction with a synergist, i.e. citric acid or phosphoric acid, which enhances its effect. It prevents rancidity and also delays flavour deterioration due to oxidation.

Effects on Health It raises the lipid and cholesterol levels in the blood. Because it encourages the formation of metabolising enzymes in the liver there is the increased risk of the breakdown of important substances in the body such as vitamin D. The Hyperactive Children's Support Group recommend that this is not included in the diet of food-sensitive children. It is not permitted in foods intended for babies or young children, with the exception of its use to preserve added vitamin A

Modified Starch Used as thickener. An umbrella term for 18 substances not defined by 'E' numbers.
Effects on Health No suggestion that they are harmful.

E472(b) Lactic Acid Esters of Mono- and Di-glycerides of Fatty Acids Used to emulsify, stabilise, and as a texture modifier.
Effects on Health No known health risks.

E475 Polyglycerol Esters of Fatty Acids Stabiliser and emulsifier.
Effects on Health No known health risks.

297 Fumaric Acid Used to flavour or acidify, and as an antioxidant and raising agent in baked goods.
Effects on Health No known health risks.

E450(a) Tetrasodium Diphosphate Maintains acidity/alkalinity at determined level. An emulsifying salt and stabiliser, also gelling agent.
Effects on Health No health risks known.

Flavourings
Effects on Health Debatable, as no information is available. Many substances in this category are artificially synthesised; safety cannot be assumed.

SAFEWAY CHEESE CAKE MIX

Sugar***   *Salt*

Modified Starch Used as thickener. An umbrella term for 18 substances not defined by 'E' numbers.
Effects on Health No suggestion that they are harmful.

E450(a) Tetrasodium Diphosphate Maintains acidity/alkalinity at determined level, an emulsifying salt and stabiliser, also gelling agent.
Effects on Health No health risk known.

E472(a) Acetic Acid Esters of Mono- and Di-glycerides of Fatty Acids Used to emulsify, stabilise, and as a texture modifier or coating agent.
Effects on Health No known health risks.

E472(b) Lactic Acid Esters of Mono- and Di-glycerides of Fatty Acids Used to emulsify, stabilise, and as a texture modifier.
Effects on Health No known health risks.

E401 Sodium Alginate Stabilises, thickens and emulsifies.
Effects on Health No known health risks.

E339 Sodium Dihydrogen Orthophosphate Used to enhance effects of other antioxidants, improve texture,

and to balance acidity/alkalinity at a determined level.
Effects on Health Not known as a health risk.

297 Fumaric Acid Used to flavour or acidify, and as an antioxidant and raising agent in baked goods.
Effects on Health Not known as a health risk.

Flavourings
Effects on Health Debatable, as no information is available. Many substances in this category are artificially synthesised; safety cannot be assumed.

E110 Sunset Yellow FCF
Gives yellow colouring to food.
Effects on Health One of the azo-dye family which is recommended to be excluded from the diets of hyperactive children. Adults may have an allergic reaction with symptoms of skin rash, swollen blood vessels and gastric problems, especially if aspirin sensitive.

E104 Quinoline Yellow Gives greenish-yellow tint to food.
Effects on Health This is a synthetic dye of the azo family and therefore is not recommended by the Hyperactive Children's Support Group for inclusion in the diets of susceptible children.

E124 Ponceau 4R Gives red colouring to food.
Effects on Health One of the azo-dye family which is recommended to be excluded from the diets of hyperactive children. Adults who are aspirin sensitive or asthmatic may be affected.

SAINSBURY'S CHEESE CAKE MIX
Sugar*** *Salt**

Modified Starch Used as thickener. An umbrella term for 18 substances not defined by 'E' numbers.
Effects on Health No suggestion that they are harmful.

E450(a) Tetrasodium Diphosphate Maintains acidity/alkalinity at determined level, an emulsifying salt and stabiliser, also gelling agent.
Effects on Health No health risks known.

E341 Calcium Hydrogen Orthophosphate Emulsifying salt used as a firming agent, to enhance the antioxidant action of other substances and maintain acidity/alkalinity at a determined level.
Effects on Health No known health risk.

E472(a) Acetic Acid Esters of Mono- and Di-glycerides of Fatty Acids Used to emulsify, stabilise, and as a texture modifier or coating agent.
Effects on Health No known health risk.

E472(b) Lactic Acid Esters of Mono- and Di-glycerides of Fatty Acids Used to emulsify, stabilise, and as a texture modifier.
Effects on Health There are no known health risks.

Flavourings
Effects on Health Debatable, as no information is available. Many substances in this category are artificially synthesised; safety cannot be assumed.

E102 Tartrazine Gives yellow colouring to food.
Effects on Health Has been implicated with causing sleeplessness at night in hyperactive and food-sensitive children. Symptoms including skin rashes, hay fever, problems with breathing, blurred vision and purple skin patches are reported in susceptible people, particularly those who are aspirin sensitive or asthmatic.

E124 Ponceau 4R Gives red colouring to food.
Effects on Health One of the azo-dye family which is recommended to be excluded from the diets of hyperactive children. Adults who are aspirin sensitive or asthmatic may be affected.

E401 Sodium Alginate Stabilises, thickens and emulsifies.
Effects on Health No known health risks.

E320 Butylated Hydroxyanisole As an antioxidant this works alone or in conjunction with a synergist, i.e. citric acid or phosphoric acid, which enhances its effect. It prevents rancidity and also delays flavour deterioration due to oxidation.
Effects on Health It raises the lipid and cholesterol levels in the blood. Because it encourages the formation of metabolising enzymes in the liver there is the increased risk of the breakdown of important substances in the body such as vitamin D. The Hyperactive Children's Support Group recommend that this is not included in the diet of food-sensitive children. It is not permitted in foods intended for babies or young children, with the exception of its use to preserve added vitamin A.

TESCO CHEESE CAKE MIX

Sugar***   *Salt*

E102 Tartrazine Gives yellow colouring to food.
Effects on Health Has been implicated with causing sleeplessness at night in hyperactive and food-sensitive children. Symptoms including skin rashes, hay fever, problems with breathing, blurred vision and purple skin patches are reported in susceptible people, particularly those who are aspirin sensitive or asthmatic.

E320 Butylated Hydroxyanisole As an antioxidant this works alone or in conjunction with a synergist, i.e. citric acid or phosphoric acid, which enhances its effect. It prevents rancidity and also delays flavour deterioration due to oxidation.
Effects on Health It raises the lipid and cholesterol levels in the blood. Because it encourages the formation of metabolising enzymes in the liver there is the increased risk of the breakdown of important substances in the body such as vitamin D. The Hyperactive Children's Support Group recommend that this is not included in the diet of food-sensitive children. It is not permitted in foods intended for babies or young children, with the exception of its use to preserve added vitamin A.

Modified Starch Used as thickener. An umbrella term for 18 substances not defined by 'E' numbers.
Effects on Health No suggestion that they are harmful.

E450(a) Tetrasodium Diphosphate Maintains acidity/alkalinity at determined level, is an emulsifying salt and stabiliser, also gelling agent.
Effects on Health No health risks known.

E401 Sodium Alginate Stabilises, thickens and emulsifies.
Effects on Health No known health risks.

E472(a) Acetic Acid Esters of Mono- and Di-glycerides of Fatty Acids Used to emulsify, stabilise, and as a texture modifier or coating agent.
Effects on Health No known health risks.

E472(b) Lactic Acid Esters of Mono- and Di-glycerides of Fatty Acids Used to emulsify, stabilise, and as a texture modifier.
Effects on Health No known health risks.

297 Fumaric Acid Used to flavour or acidify, and as an antioxidant and raising agent in baked goods.
Effects on Health Not known as a health risk.

E102 Tartrazine Gives yellow colouring to food.
Effects on Health Has been implicated with causing sleeplessness at night in hyperactive and food-sensitive children. Symptoms including skin rashes, hay fever, problems with breathing, blurred vision and purple skin patches are reported in susceptible people.

E124 Ponceau 4R Gives red colouring to food.
Effects on Health One of the azo-dye family which is recommended to be excluded from the diets of hyperactive children. Adults who are aspirin sensitive or asthmatic may be affected.

Cheese Sauce Mix

SUPERCOOK CHEESE SAUCE MIX

Sugar*   Salt**

Edible Starch Used as thickener. An umbrella term for 18 substances not defined by 'E' numbers.
Effects on Health No suggestion that they are harmful.

Flavourings
Effects on Health Debatable, as no information is available. Many substances in this category are artificially synthesised; safety cannot be assumed.

621 Monosodium Glutamate Enhances the flavour of foods containing protein by stimulating the taste buds or increasing degree of saliva produced in the mouth.
Effects on Health Responsible for symptoms of palpitation, headache, dizziness, nausea, muscle tightness, a feeling of weakness in the forearms, pains in the neck, and other, migraine-like symptoms in some people. This substance is recommended to be excluded from the diets of hyperactive children; it is also taboo in or on foods intended for babies and young children.

554 Aluminium Sodium Silicate Used to prevent particles sticking together.
Effects on Health Some people react to aluminium, and others should avoid excessive sodium intake, so not entirely free of health hazard.

SAINSBURY'S CHEESE SAUCE MIX

Sugar*   Salt**

Starch Used as thickener. An umbrella term for 18 substances not defined by 'E' numbers.
Effects on Health No suggestion that they are harmful.

E320 Butylated Hydroxyanisole As an antioxidant this works alone or in conjunction with a synergist, i.e. citric acid or phosphoric acid, which enhances the effect. It prevents rancidity and also delays flavour deterioration due to oxidation.
Effects on Health It raises the lipid and cholesterol levels in the blood. Because it encourages the formation of metabolising enzymes in the liver, there is the increased risk of the breakdown of important substances in the body such as vitamin D. The

Hyperactive Children's Support Group recommend that this is not included in the diet of food-sensitive children. It is not permitted in foods intended for babies and young children with the exception of its use to preserve added Vitamin A.

Flavourings
Effects on Health Debatable, as no information is available. Many substances in this category are artificially synthesised; safety cannot be assumed.

621 Monosodium Glutamate
Enhances the flavour of foods containing protein by stimulating the taste buds or increasing degree of saliva produced in the mouth.
Effects on Health Responsible for symptoms of palpitation, headache, dizziness, nausea, muscle tightness, a feeling of weakness in the forearms, pains in the neck, and other, migraine-like symptoms in some people. This substance is recommended to be excluded from the diets of hyperactive children; it is also taboo in or on foods intended for babies and young children.

E340(a) Potassium Dihydrogen Orthophosphate
Emulsifying salt used as firming agent; used also to enhance the antioxidant action of other substances and maintain acidity/alkalinity at a determined level.
Effects on Health Not known as a health risk.

E471 Mono- and Di-Glycerides of Fatty Acids
Used to emulsify and stabilise.
Effects on Health Not known as a health risk.

E472(b) Lactic Acid Esters of Mono- and Di-Glycerides of Fatty Acids
Used to emulsify, stabilise, and as a texture modifier.
Effects on Health There are no known health risks.

SAFEWAY CHEESE SAUCE MIX
Sugar   Salt**

621 Monosodium Glutamate
Enhances the flavour of foods containing protein by stimulating the taste buds or increasing degree of saliva produced in the mouth.
Effects on Health Responsible for symptoms of palpitation, headache, dizziness, nausea, muscle tightness, a feeling of weakness in the forearms, pains in the neck, and other, migraine-like symptoms in some people. This substance is recommended to be excluded from the diets of hyperactive children; it is also taboo in or on foods intended for babies and young children.

Flavour
Effects on Health Debatable, as no information is available.

Many substances in this category are artificially synthesised; safety cannot be assumed.

E471 Mono- and Di-Glycerides of Fatty Acids
Used to emulsify and stabilise.
Effects on Health Not known as a health risk.

296 Malic Acid Gives flavouring, an acid derived from apples.
Effects on Health No known health risk.

E102 Tartrazine Gives yellow colouring to food.
Effects on Health Has been implicated with causing sleeplessness at night in hyperactive and food-sensitive children. Symptoms including skin rashes, hay fever, problems with breathing, blurred vision and purple skin patches are reported in susceptible people, particularly those who are aspirin sensitive or asthmatic.

E110 Sunset Yellow FCF
Gives yellow colouring to food.
Effects on Health One of the azo-dye family which is recommended to be excluded from the diets of hyperactive children. Adults may have an allergic reaction with symptoms of skin rash, swollen blood vessels and gastric problems, especially if aspirin sensitive.

E124 Ponceau 4R Gives red colouring to food.
Effects on Health One of the azo-dye family which is recommended to be excluded from the diets of hyperactive children. Adults who are aspirin sensitive or asthmatic may be affected.

KNORR CHEESE SAUCE MIX

Sugar*   *Salt***

Starch Used as thickener. An umbrella term for 18 substances not defined by 'E' numbers.
Effects on Health No suggestion that they are harmful.

E320 Butylated Hydroxyanisole
As an antioxidant this works alone or in conjunction with a synergist, i.e. citric acid or phosphoric acid, which enhances its effect. It prevents rancidity and also delays flavour deterioration due to oxidation.
Effects on Health It raises the lipid and cholesterol levels in the blood. Because it encourages the formation of metabolising enzymes in the liver, there is the increased risk of the breakdown of important substances in the body such as vitamin D. The Hyperactive Children's Support Group recommend that this is not included in the diet of food-sensitive children. It is not permitted in foods intended for babies and young children with the exception of its use to preserve added Vitamin A.

621 Monosodium Glutamate

Enhances the flavour of foods containing protein by stimulating the taste buds or increasing degree of saliva produced in the mouth.

Effects on Health Responsible for symptoms of palpitation, headache, dizziness, nausea, muscle tightness, a feeling of weakness in the forearms, pains in the neck, and other, migraine-like symptoms in some people. This substance is recommended to be excluded from the diets of hyperactive children; it is also taboo in or on foods intended for babies and young children.

Flavour

Effects on Health Debatable, as no information is available. Many substances in this category are artificially synthesised; safety cannot be assumed.

E340(a) Potassium Dihydrogen Orthophosphate

Emulsifying salt used as firming agent; used also to enhance the antioxidant action of other substances and maintain acidity/alkalinity at a determined level.

Effects on Health Not known as a health risk.

E471 Mono- and Di-Glycerides of Fatty Acids

Used to emulsify and stabilise.

Effects on Health Not known as a health risk.

E472(b) Lactic Acid Esters of Mono- and Di-Glycerides of Fatty Acids

Used to emulsify, stabilise, and as a texture modifier.

Effects on Health There are no known health risks.

E102 Tartrazine

Gives yellow colouring to food.

Effects on Health Has been implicated with causing sleeplessness at night in hyperactive and food-sensitive children. Symptoms including skin rashes, hay fever, problems with breathing, blurred vision and purple skin patches are reported in susceptible people, particularly those who are aspirin sensitive or asthmatic.

E110 Sunset Yellow FCF

Gives yellow colouring to food.

Effects on Health One of the azo-dye family which is recommended to be excluded from the diets of hyperactive children. Adults may have an allergic reaction with symptoms of skin rash, swollen blood vessels and gastric problems, especially if aspirin sensitive.

E124 Ponceau 4R

Gives red colouring to food.

Effects on Health One of the azo-dye family which is recommended to be excluded from the diets of hyperactive children. Adults who are aspirin sensitive or asthmatic may be affected.

Cheese Spreads

THE LAUGHING COW CHEESE SPREAD

Sugar   Salt

'Emulsifying Salts'
Yet to be specified, but possibly
E450(a), **E450(b)** or **E450(c)**.
Effects on Health With (b) and
(c) there is research work from
France to suggest that
polyphosphates block certain
enzymes, causing digestive
disturbances. There is no health
risk with 450(a).

similar

FINE FARE CHEESE SPREAD

also

SAFEWAY CHEESE SPREAD

TESCO CHEESE SPREAD, NATURAL

Sugar   Salt

**E450(a) Tetrasodium
Diphosphate** Maintains
acidity/alkalinity at determined
level; an emulsifying salt and
stabiliser, also gelling agent.

Effects on Health No health risks
known.

**E450(b) Pentasodium
Triphosphate** Used to provide
texture and is an emulsifying
salt.
Effects on Health French research
suggests that polyphosphates can
block a number of enzymes,
causing digestive disturbances.

**E450(c) Sodium
Polyphosphates** Emulsifying
salts, used to stabilise.
Effects on Health French research
suggests that polyphosphates
might block a number of
enzymes, causing digestive
disturbances.

E234 Nisin Used to preserve.
Effects on Health There are no
known health risks.

CO-OP CHEESE SPREAD

Sugar   Salt

**E339 Sodium Dihydrogen
Orthophosphate** Used to
enhance the effects of other
antioxidants, as a texture
improver and to balance
acidity/alkalinity at a
determined level.
Effects on Health There are no
known health risks.

E450(a) Tetrasodium Diphosphate Maintains acidity/alkalinity at determined level; an emulsifying salt and stabiliser, also gelling agent. *Effects on Health* No health risks known.

E450(c) Sodium Polyphosphates Emulsifying salts, used to stabilise. *Effects on Health* French research suggests that polyphosphates might block a number of enzymes, causing digestive disturbances.

E234 Nisin Used to preserve. *Effects on Health* There are no known health risks.

E200 Sorbic Acid A preservative, and an inhibitor of yeast and mould growth. *Effects on Health* Possibility of irritating skin.

ST IVEL FAMILY FAVOURITES
Sugar   Salt

'Emulsifying Salts' Yet to be specified, but possibly **E450(a), E450(b), E450(c)** or **E339. E450(a) Tetrasodium Diphosphate** Maintains acidity/alkalinity at determined level; an emulsifying salt and stabiliser, also gelling agent. *Effects on Health* No known health risk.

E450(b) Pentasodium Triphosphate Used to provide texture and is an emulsifying salt. *Effects on Health* French research suggests that polyphosphates can block a number of enzymes, causing digestive disturbances.

E450(c) Sodium Polyphosphates Emulsifying salts, used to stabilise. *Effects on Health* French research suggests that polyphosphates might block a number of enzymes, causing digestive disturbances.

E339 Sodium Dihydrogen Orthophosphate Used to enhance effects of other antioxidants, as a texture improver and to balance acidity/alkalinity at a determined level. *Effects on Health* There are no known health risks.

'Colours' These will have to be specified from 1986, and could include **E100 Curcumin** or **E101 Riboflavin** (both giving yellow-orange colour to product) which carry no health risk.

or **E102 Tartrazine** or **E110 Sunset Yellow FCF** (also giving yellow colour to product) which are both members of the azo-dye family which carry risks of adversely affecting those who are sensitive to aspirin or are asthmatic; they are not recommended to be included in the diets of hyperactive children. *Effects on Health* Therefore depend crucially on which colours are included.

Chicken Casserole Mixes

HOMEPRIDE COOK-IN SAUCE CHICKEN CHASSEUR

Sugar**   *Salt***

Modified Starch Used as thickener. An umbrella term for 18 substances not defined by 'E' numbers.
Effects on Health No suggestion that they are harmful.

COLMAN'S COQ AU VIN

Sugar   *Salt***

621 Monosodium Glutamate Enhances the flavour of foods containing protein by stimulating the taste buds or increasing degree of saliva produced in the mouth.
Effects on Health Responsible for symptoms of palpitation, muscle tightness, headache, dizziness, nausea, a feeling of weakness in the forearms, pains in the neck, and other, migraine-like symptoms in some people. This substance is recommended to be excluded from the diets of hyperactive children; it is also taboo in or on foods intended for babies and young children.

E334 Tartaric Acid Used as an antioxidant either alone or as a synergist, i.e. to enhance the antioxidant effect of other substances.
Effects on Health No known health risk except as an irritant if taken in very large quantities.

'Colours' will have to be specified from 1986 and might include **E150 Caramel** which gives a brown colour to product and is also used as a flavouring.
Effects on Health A question mark as to its safety hangs over this additive. There has been a reduction in the number of kinds available to the food industry. Work is in hand to discover the safest form. One type which is produced with ammonia has been shown to cause vitamin B6 deficiency in rats.

'Colours' might also include **E155 Brown HT** or **E124 Ponceau 4R** Both are azo-dyes and therefore recommended to be excluded from the diets of hyperactive children. They may also cause adverse reactions in adults who are aspirin sensitive or who suffer from asthma or skin allergy.

Flavours
Effects on Health Debatable, as
no information is available.
Many substances in this
category are artificially
synthesised; safety cannot be
assumed.

FINE FARE CHICKEN CHASSEUR
Sugar**   *Salt***

621 Monosodium Glutamate
Enhances the flavour of foods
containing protein by
stimulating the taste buds or
increasing degree of saliva
produced in the mouth.
Effects on Health Responsible for
symptoms of palpitation,
headache, dizziness, nausea,
muscle tightness, a feeling of
weakness in the forearms, pains
in the neck, and other,
migraine-like symptoms in some
people. This substance is
recommended to be excluded
from the diets of hyperactive
children; it is also taboo in or
on foods intended for babies and
young children.

E150 Caramel Gives a brown
colour to product and is used as a
flavouring.
Effects on Health A question
mark as to its safety hangs over
this additive. There has been a
reduction in the number of
kinds available to the food
industry. Work is in hand to

discover the safest form. One
type which is produced with
ammonia has been shown to
cause vitamin B6 deficiency in
rats.

E155 Brown HT Gives brown
colouring to product.
Effects on Health As a member of
the azo-dye family this should
be avoided by those who suffer
from aspirin sensitivity, are
asthmatic or have a tendency to
allergies. It is recommended to
be excluded from the diets of
hyperactive children by the
Hyperactive Children's Support
Group.

E124 Ponceau 4R Gives red
colouring to product.
Effects on Health One of the azo-
dye family which is
recommended to be excluded
from the diets of hyperactive
children. Adults who are aspirin
sensitive or asthmatic may be
affected.

CROSSE & BLACKWELL COOK-IN-THE-POT CHICKEN CHASSEUR
Sugar**   *Salt***

Modified Starch Used as
thickener. An umbrella term for
18 substances not defined by 'E'
numbers.
Effects on Health No suggestion
that they are harmful.

Flavouring
Effects on Health Debatable, as
no information is available.
Many substances in this
category are artificially
synthesised; safety cannot be
assumed.

621 Monosodium Glutamate
Enhances the flavour of foods
containing protein by
stimulating the taste buds or
increasing degree of saliva
produced in the mouth.
Effects on Health Responsible for
symptoms of palpitation,
headache, dizziness, nausea,
muscle tightness, a feeling of
weakness in the forearms, pains
in the neck, and other,
migraine-like symptoms in some
people. This substance is
recommended to be excluded
from the diets of hyperactive
children; it is also taboo in or
on foods intended for babies and
young children.

E150 Caramel Gives a brown
colouring to product and is used
as flavouring.

Effects on Health A question
mark as to its safety hangs over
this additive. There has been a
reduction in the number of
kinds available to the food
industry. Work is in hand to
discover the safest form. One
kind which is produced with
ammonia has been shown to
cause vitamin B6 deficiency in
rats.

'Colour' Possibly **E155 Brown
HT** or **E124 Ponceau 4R** Both
are members of the azo-dye
family which are recommended
to be excluded from the diets of
hyperactive children. Adults
who are allergy prone,
asthmatics or aspirin-sensitive
may also be affected.

E330 Citric Acid Stabilises the
acidity of food substances,
prevents discoloration of fruit,
keeps the flavour 'true' and
retains vitamin C.
Effects on Health Needs to be
consumed in very large
quantities to erode teeth or
irritate locally.

Chocolate Mousse

CHAMBOURCY
CHOCOLATE MOUSSE
Sugar**   *Salt*

**E471 Mono- and Di-
glycerides of Fatty Acids** An
emulsifier and stabiliser.
Effects on Health Not known as a
health risk.

E331 Sodium Citrates Acts as
a synergist, i.e. enhances the
effects of other antioxidants, is an
emulsifying salt and controls the
acid/alkaline level.
Effects on Health No known
health risk.

ST IVEL CHOCOLATE SOUFFLÉ

Sugar***   *Salt*

Modified Starch Used as thickener. An umbrella term for 18 substances not defined by 'E' numbers.
Effects on Health No suggestion that they are harmful.

'Emulsifiers' Yet to be specified, possibly **E471 Mono- and Di-glycerides of Fatty Acids** An emulsifier and stabiliser.
Effects on Health Not known as a health risk.

Flavouring
Effects on Health Debatable, as no information is available. Many substances in this category are artificially synthesised; safety cannot be assumed.

'Colour' Possibly **E102, E110** or **E122**, but will be specified from 1986.
Effects on Health As members of the azo-dye family, these are synthetic colours which are not recommended to be included in the diet of hyperactive children. They may also provoke adverse reactions in those who suffer from asthma or are aspirin sensitive.

'Stabiliser' Yet to be specified. This could be one of many permitted substances.
Effects on Health Few of these have any known health hazard associated with them.

also

BIRD'S EYE SUPERMOUSSE

ROSS CHOCOLATE MOUSSE

Sugar***   *Salt*

E412 Guar Gum A thickener or bulking agent.
Effects on Health Harmless except in excess when stomach cramps, nausea and flatulence might result.

E407 Carrageenan Used to thicken, emulsify, or as a gelling agent.
Effects on Health It has been reported as a possible cause of ulcerative colitis and when degraded may be carcinogenic. The most harmful form is that taken in drink.

E471 Mono- and Di-glycerides of Fatty Acids An emulsifier and stabiliser.
Effects on Health Not known as a health risk.

E433 Polyoxethylene Used to emulsify and stabilise.
Effects on Health Not known as a health risk.

E155 Brown HT Gives a brown colour to food.
Effects on Health As a member of

the azo-dye family such synthetic dyes are recommended to be excluded from the diets of hyperactive children; they may also be harmful to those who suffer from asthma or are aspirin sensitive.

E123 Amaranth Gives a red colour to food.
Effects on Health As an azo-dye it should be avoided by people who are sensitive to aspirin as it may cause a skin rash. The Hyperactive Children's Support Group recommend it is excluded from the diets of food-sensitive children.

E142 Acid Brilliant Green Gives a green colour to food.
Effects on Health No ill effects are reported, except, as a synthetic dye, it may affect hyperactive children and those who suffer from asthma or who are aspirin sensitive.

SAFEWAY CHOCOLATE MOUSSE
Sugar***   *Salt*

Flavouring
Effects on Health Debatable, as no information is available. Many substances in this category are artificially synthesised; safety cannot be assumed.

E471 Mono- and Di-glycerides of Fatty Acids An emulsifier and stabiliser.

Effects on Health Not known as a health risk.

E407 Carrageenan Used to thicken, emulsify, or as a gelling agent.
Effects on Health There are reports that this is a possible cause of ulcerative colitis and when degraded may be carcinogenic. The most harmful form is that taken in drink.

E410 Locust Bean Gum Used to stabilise and emulsify, also a gelling agent.
Effects on Health There are no known health risks. Pods of the bean have been consumed since Biblical times.

E102 Tartrazine Gives a yellow colour to food.
Effects on Health Has been implicated in causing sleeplessness at night in hyperactive and food-sensitive children. Symptoms including skin rashes, hay fever, problems with breathing, blurred vision and purple skin patches are reported in susceptible people, particularly those who are aspirin sensitive and asthmatic.

E110 Sunset Yellow FCF Gives a yellow colour to food.
Effects on Health One of the azo-dye family which is recommended to be excluded from the diets of hyperactive children. Adults may have an allergic reaction with symptoms of skin rash, swollen blood vessels and gastric problems, especially if aspirin sensitive.

E122 Carmoisine Gives a red colour to food.
Effects on Health This has been recommended by the Hyperactive Children's Support Group as unsuitable for children who are food sensitive. An azo-dye, it may produce adverse reactions in those people who have aspirin allergy or are asthmatic. Such reactions can include skin rashes or swelling.

E141 Copper Complexes of Chlorophyll and Chlorophyllins Gives a green colour to food.
Effects on Health There are no known risks.

Chocolate Sponge Mix

SAINSBURY'S CHOCOLATE SPONGE MIX
Sugar *   *Salt*

E471 Mono- and Di-Glycerides of Fatty Acids Used to emulsify or stabilise.
Effects on Health No known health risks.

500 Sodium Bicarbonate Used to balance alkaline/acid levels and to aerate.
Effects on Health Not known as a health risk.

541 Sodium Aluminium Phosphate Used as a raising agent for flour; acid.
Effects on Health Because sodium is related to the water balance of the body an intake to excess can be dangerous. Those at highest risk are sufferers of heart and kidney complaints, and small babies. A few people also react adversely to aluminium.

Flavouring
Effects on Health Debatable, as no information is available. Many substances in this category are artificially synthesised; safety cannot be assumed.

VIOTA CHOCOLATE FUDGE CAKE MIX
Sugar ***   *Salt* *

500 Sodium Bicarbonate Used to balance alkaline/acid levels and to aerate.
Effects on Health Not known as a health risk.

541 Sodium Aluminium Phosphate Used as a raising agent for flour; acid.
Effects on Health Because sodium is related to the water balance of the body an intake to excess can be dangerous. Those at highest risk are sufferers of heart and kidney complaints, and small babies. A few people also react adversely to aluminium.

E471 Mono- and Di-Glycerides of Fatty Acids
Used to emulsify or stabilise.
Effects on Health No known
health risk.

Flavouring
Effects on Health Debatable, as
no information is available.
Many substances in this
category are artificially
synthesised; safety cannot be
assumed.

**E466
Carboxymethylcellulose,
Sodium Salt** Used to modify
texture, to thicken, stabilise and
add bulk, and is a gelling agent.
Effects on Health There is a
suggestion that there is a
possibility of intestinal
obstruction but, generally, no
risk.

GREEN'S BAVARIAN CHOCOLATE SPONGE SANDWICH MIX
Sugar***   *Salt**

500 Sodium Bicarbonate
Used to balance alkaline/acid
levels and to aerate.
Effects on Health Not known as a
health risk.

**541 Sodium Aluminium
Phosphate** Used as a raising
agent for flour; acid.
Effects on Health Because sodium
is related to the water balance
of the body an intake to excess
can be dangerous. Those at

highest risk are sufferers of heart
and kidney complaints, and
small babies. A few people also
react adversely to aluminium.

**E450(a) Tetrasodium
Diphosphate** Maintains
acidity/alkalinity at a
determined level; an emulsifying
salt and stabiliser, also gelling
agent.
Effects on Health No health risks
known.

Modified Starch Used as
thickener. An umbrella term for
18 substances not defined by 'E'
numbers.
Effects on Health No suggestion
that they are harmful.

E150 Caramel Gives brown
colour to product and is used as
a flavouring.
Effects on Health A question
mark as to its safety hangs over
this additive. There has been a
reduction in the number of
kinds available to the food
industry. Work is in hand to
discover the safest form. One
kind which is produced with
ammonia has been shown to
cause vitamin B6 deficiency in
rats.

E123 Amaranth Gives red
colour to product.
Effects on Health As an azo-dye it
should be avoided by people
who are sensitive to aspirin as it
may cause a skin rash. The
Hyperactive Children's Support
Group recommend it is
excluded from the diets of food-
sensitive children.

E471 Mono- and Di-glycerides of Fatty Acids
Used to emulsify or stabilise.
Effects on Health No known health risks.

E475 Polyglycerol Esters of Fatty Acids Used to emulsify or stabilise.
Effects on Health No known health risk.

E341 Calcium Tetrahydrogen Diorthophosphate Used to maintain alkalinity/acidity at a determined level, to prevent softening of fruit during processing; an emulsifying salt and raising agent, enhances action of other antioxidants.
Effects on Health No known health risks.

Flavourings
Effects on Health Debatable, as no information is available. Many substances in this category are artificially synthesised; safety cannot be assumed.

E320 Butylated Hydroxyanisole As an antioxidant this works alone or in conjunction with a synergist, i.e. citric acid or phosphoric acid, which enhances its effect. It prevents rancidity and also delays flavour deterioration due to oxidation.
Effects on Health It raises the lipid and cholesterol levels in the blood. Because it encourages the formation of metabolising enzymes in the liver there is the risk of the breakdown of important substances in the body such as vitamin D. The Hyperactive Children's Support Group recommend that this is not included in the diet of food-sensitive children. It is not permitted in foods intended for babies and young children with the exception of its use to preserve added vitamin A.

GRANNY SMITH'S CHOCOLATE SANDWICH CAKE MIX
Sugar*** Salt*

E471 Mono- and Di-Glycerides of Fatty Acids
Used to emulsify or stabilise.
Effects on Health No known health risk.

E320 Butylated Hydroxyanisole As an antioxidant this works alone or in conjunction with a synergist, i.e. citric acid or phosphoric acid, which enhances its effect. It prevents rancidity and also delays flavour deterioration due to oxidation.
Effects on Health It raises the lipid and cholesterol levels in the blood. Because it encourages the formation of metabolising enzymes in the liver there is the risk of the breakdown of important substances in the body such as vitamin D. The Hyperactive Children's Support Group recommend that this is not included in the diet of food-sensitive children. It is not

permitted in foods intended for babies and young children with the exception of its use to preserve added Vitamin A.

575 Glucono-delta-lactone

Delays oxidation process and premature setting of dessert mixes; emulsifies. In the dairy industry, prevents deposits of magnesium and calcium phosphates when milk is heated to high temperature.
Effects on Health Not known as a health risk.

E150 Caramel Gives brown

colour to product and is used as a flavouring.
Effects on Health A question mark as to its safety hangs over this additive. There has been a reduction in the number of kinds available to the food industry. Work is in hand to discover the safest form. One kind which is produced with ammonia has been shown to cause vitamin B6 deficiency in rats.

E110 Sunset Yellow FCF

Gives yellow colour to product.
Effects on Health One of the azo-dye family which is recommended to be excluded from the diets of hyperactive children. Adults may have an allergic reaction with symptoms of skin rash, swollen blood vessels and gastric problems, especially if aspirin sensitive.

E124 Ponceau 4R Gives red

colour to product.
Effects on Health One of the azo-dye family which is recommended to be excluded from the diets of hyperactive children. Adults who are aspirin sensitive or asthmatic may be affected.

E142 Acid Brilliant Green

Gives green colour to product.
Effects on Health No ill effects reported although as a synthetic azo-dye it may affect hyperactive children and those who suffer from asthma or are aspirin sensitive.

Flavourings

Effects on Health Debatable, as no information is available. Many substances in this category are artificially synthesised; safety cannot be assumed.

E415 Xanthan Gum Used to

stabilise, emulsify or thicken.
Effects on Health No serious health risks, but heavy consumption could cause abdominal pain and distension.

E341 Calcium Tetrahydrogen Diorthophosphate Used to

maintain alkalinity/acidity at a determined level, to prevent softening of fruit during processing, as emulsifying salt and raising agent; enhances the action of other antioxidants.
Effects on Health No known health risk.

Chocolate Sponge Pudding

HEINZ

*Sugar*** *Salt*

E450(a) Disodium Dihydrogen Diphosphate
Used to emulsify as a raising agent for flour and to improve colour; maintains the acidity/alkalinity pH at a determined level.
Effects on Health No known ill effects.

500 Sodium Bicarbonate
Used to increase alkalinity or reduce acidity; to aerate.
Effects on Health No health risks known.

CO-OP

*Sugar**** *Salt***

Flavourings
Effects on Health Debatable, as no information is available. Many substances in this category are artificially synthesised; safety cannot be assumed.

ST MICHAEL

*Sugar**** *Salt****

E415 Xanthan Gum Used to stabilise, thicken and emulsify.
Effects on Health No serious health risks, but heavy consumption could cause abdominal pain and distension.

E410 Locust Bean Gum Used to emulsify, stabilise; a gelling agent.
Effects on Health No known health risk. Pods of the bean have been eaten since Biblical times. Heavy consumption of the gum could, however, cause stomach pain and swelling.

E412 Guar Gum Used to thicken, as a dietary bulking agent, and to stabilise emulsions.
Effects on Health Harmless except when eaten in very large quantities when stomach cramps, nausea and flatulence might occur.

E150 Caramel Gives brown colour to product and is used as a flavouring.
Effects on Health A question mark as to its safety hangs over this additive. There has been a reduction in the number of

kinds available to the food
industry. Work is in hand to
discover the safest form. One
kind which is produced with
ammonia has been shown to
cause vitamin B6 deficiency in
rats.

E155 Brown HT Used to give
a brown colour to product.

Effects on Health People who are
asthmatic or have a sensitivity
to aspirin should avoid this azo-
dye, as should those who have a
skin sensitivity. This colour
appears on the list of substances
which the Hyperactive
Children's Support Group
recommend be excluded from
food-sensitive children's diets.

Chocolate Wafer and Sandwich Biscuits

FOXE'S TRIPLE SANDWICH BISCUITS WITH CHOCOLATE FILLING

Sugar***   *Salt***

'Emulsifier' One of a large
class of permitted substances
which will have to be specified
after January 1986.
Effects on Health Few members of
this class present any health
hazard.

TWIX

Sugar***   *Salt***

500 Sodium Bicarbonate
Used to balance alkaline/acid
levels and to aerate.
Effects on Health Not known as a
health risk.

Flavourings
Effects on Health Debatable, as
no information is available.
Many substances in this
category are artificially
synthesised; safety cannot be
assumed.

Plus (for Safeway)
E322 Lecithin Acts as an
emulsifier and stabiliser, is an
antioxidant and gives additional
thickness to fats.
Effects on Health There are no
known health risks; in fact,
lecithin is used therapeutically
to mobilise fat in the body and
has also been experimented with
in the treatment of senile
dementia.

also

SAFEWAY CHOCOLATE FINGER WAFERS

Sugar**   *Salt**

PENGUIN CHOCOLATE SANDWICH
Sugar***   *Salt**

E150 Caramel Gives brown colouring to product and is used as a flavouring.
Effects on Health A question mark as to its safety hangs over this additive. There has been a reduction in the number of kinds available to the food industry. Work is in hand to discover the safest form. One kind which is produced with ammonia has been shown to cause vitamin B6 deficiency in rats.

E127 Erythrosine gives red colouring to product. A coal tar dye.
Effects on Health This additive can cause sensitivity to light and has also been recommended by the Hyperactive Children's Support Group to be excluded from the diets of hyperactive children. Because it contains 577mg of iodine per gram there is a risk that the consuming of a number of foods which contain E127 might cause an overactive thyroid.

500 Sodium Bicarbonate Used to balance alkaline/acid levels and to aerate.
Effects on Health Not known as a health risk.

503 Ammonium Carbonate Used to maintain the alkaline/acid pH at a determined level; to aerate.

Effects on Health Not known as a health risk.

E322 Lecithin Acts as an emulsifier, stabilises; it is an antioxidant that gives additional thickness to fats.
Effects on Health There are no known health risks; in fact, lecithin is used therapeutically to mobilise fat in the body and has also been experimented with in the treatment of senile dementia.

Flavourings
Effects on Health Debatable, as no information is available. Many substances in this category are artificially synthesised; safety cannot be assumed.

SAINSBURY'S 6's PLAIN CHOCOLATE SANDWICH BAR
Sugar**   *Salt***

E150 Caramel Gives brown colouring to product and is used as a flavouring.
Effects on Health A question mark as to its safety hangs over this additive. There has been a reduction in the number of kinds available to the food industry. Work is in hand to discover the safest form. One kind is produced with ammonia which has been shown to cause vitamin B6 deficiency in rats.

E102 Tartrazine Gives yellow
colouring to product.
Effects on Health Has been
implicated with causing
sleeplessness at night in
hyperactive and food-sensitive
children. Symptoms including
skin rashes, hay fever, problems
with breathing, blurred vision
and purple skin patches are
reported in susceptible people,
particularly those who are
aspirin sensitive or asthmatic.

E110 Sunset Yellow FCF
Gives yellow colouring to
product.
Effects on Health One of the azo-
dye family which is
recommended to be excluded
from the diets of hyperactive
children. Adults may have an
allergic reaction with symptoms
of skin rash, swollen blood
vessels and gastric problems,
especially if aspirin sensitive.

Flavouring
Effects on Health Debatable, as
no information is available.

Many substances in this
category are artificially
synthesised; safety cannot be
assumed.

**E320 Butylated
Hydroxyanisole** As an
antioxidant this works alone or
in conjunction with a synergist,
i.e. citric acid or phosphoric
acid, which enhances its effect.
It prevents rancidity and also
delays flavour deterioration due
to oxidation.
Effects on Health It raises the
lipid and cholesterol levels in
the blood. Because it encourages
the formation of metabolising
enzymes in the liver, there is the
increased risk of the breakdown
of important substances in the
body such as vitamin D. The
Hyperactive Children's Support
Group recommend that this is
not included in the diet of food-
sensitive children. It is not
permitted in foods intended for
babies and young children with
the exception of its use to
preserve added vitamin A.

Coffee Whiteners

SAINSBURY'S COFFEE WHITENER
*Sugar*** *   Salt*

**E340 Potassium
Dihydrogen
Orthophosphate** Used to
maintain acidity/alkalinity

at a determined level; an
emulsifying salt, enhances
the action of other
antioxidants.
Effects on Health No
known health risk.

E471 Mono- and Di-glycerides of Fatty Acids
An emulsifier and stabiliser.
Effects on Health Not known as a health risk.

554 Aluminium Sodium Silicate Used to prevent particles sticking together.
Effects on Health Some people react to aluminium, and others should avoid excessive sodium intake; so not entirely free of health risk.

E160(b) Annatto Bixin Norbixin Gives yellow to peach colour to product.
Effects on Health Safe except for reports of hives in some people.

also

SAFEWAY COFFEEBREAK

CARNATION COFFEEMATE

Sugar**   *Salt*

E340 Potassium Dihydrogen Orthophosphate Used to maintain alkalinity/acidity at a determined level; an emulsifying salt, enhances action of other antioxidants.
Effects on Health Not known as a health risk.

E471 Mono- and Di-glycerides of Fatty Acids An emulsifier and stabiliser.
Effects on Health Not known as a health risk.

E472(e) Mono- and Diacetyltartaric Acid Esters of Mono- and Di-glycerides of Fatty Acids An emulsifier and stabiliser.
Effects on Health No known health risk.

Flavourings
Effects on Health Debatable, as no information is available. Many substances in this category are artificially synthesised; safety cannot be assumed.

E102 Tartrazine Gives yellow colouring to product.
Effects on Health Has been implicated with causing sleeplessness at night in hyperactive and food-sensitive children. Symptoms including skin rashes, hay fever, problems with breathing, blurred vision and purple skin patches are reported in susceptible people, particularly those who are aspirin sensitive or asthmatic.

E110 Sunset Yellow FCF Gives yellow colouring to product.
Effects on Health One of the azo-dye family which is recommended to be excluded from the diets of hyperactive children. Adults may have an allergic reaction with symptoms of skin rash, swollen blood vessels and gastric problems, especially if aspirin sensitive.

also

TESCO COFFEE WHITENER

CO-OP COFFEE WHITE

*Sugar*** *Salt*

E339 Sodium Dihydrogen Orthophosphate Used to enhance effects of other antioxidants, as a texture improver and to balance acidity/alkalinity at a determined level.
Effects on Health Not known as a health risk.

E471 Mono- and Di-glycerides of Fatty Acids An emulsifier and stabiliser.
Effects on Health Not known as a health risk.

E450(c) Sodium Polyphosphates Emulsifying salts used to stabilise.
Effects on Health French research suggests that polyphosphates might block a number of enzymes, causing digestive disturbances.

E322 Lecithin Acts as an emulsifier and stabiliser; it is an antioxidant and gives additional thickness to fats.
Effects on Health There are no known health risks; in fact, lecithin is used therapeutically to mobilise fats in the body and has also been experimented with in the treatment of senile dementia.

E340 Potassium Dihydrogen Orthophosphate Used to maintain alkalinity/acidity at a determined level; an emulsifying salt, enhances the action of other antioxidants.
Effects on Health Not known as a health risk.

554 Aluminium Sodium Silicate Used to prevent particles sticking together.
Effects on Health Some people react to aluminium, and others should avoid excessive sodium; so not entirely free of health risks.

E102 Tartrazine gives yellow colouring to product.
Effects on Health Has been implicated with causing sleeplessness at night in hyperactive and food-sensitive children. Symptoms including skin rashes, hay fever, problems with breathing, blurred vision and purple skin patches are reported in susceptible people, particularly those who are aspirin sensitive or asthmatic.

E110 Sunset Yellow FCF Gives yellow colouring to product.
Effects on Health One of the azo-dye family which is recommended to be excluded from the diets of hyperactive children. Adults may have an allergic reaction with symptoms of skin rash, swollen blood vessels and gastric problems, especially if aspirin sensitive.

Cola Drinks

COCA COLA
*Sugar*** *Salt*

E150 Caramel Gives brown colour to product and is used as a flavouring.
Effects on Health A question mark as to its safety hangs over this additive. There has been a reduction in the number of kinds available to the food industry. Work is in hand to discover the safest form. One kind which is produced with ammonia has been shown to cause vitamin B6 deficiency in rats.

E338 Phosphoric Acid Has a synergist effect, enhances the antioxidant effect of other substances; used as a flavouring.
Effects on Health No known health risk, in the small quantities used in food.

Flavourings
Effects on Health Debatable, as no information is available. Many substances in this category are artificially synthesised; safety cannot be assumed.

DIET PEPSI
Sugar   *Salt*

E150 Caramel Gives brown colour to product and is used as a flavouring.
Effects on Health A question mark as to its safety hangs over this additive. There has been a reduction in the number of kinds available to the food industry. Work is in hand to discover the safest form. One kind which is produced with ammonia has been shown to cause vitamin B6 deficiency in rats.

E338 Phosphoric Acid Has a synergist effect, enhances the antioxidant effect of other substances; used as a flavouring.
Effects on Health No known health risk, in the small quantities used in food.

E414 Gum Arabic Used to thicken, emulsify and stabilise.
Effects on Health There is an occasional hypersensitivity in some people after eating this or breathing it in. Consumption of large quantities could cause stomach pain and swelling.
Flavouring
Effects on Health Debatable, as no information is available. Many substances in this category are artificially synthesised; safety cannot be assumed.

WAITROSE COLA
*Sugar*** *Salt*

E150 Caramel Gives brown colour to product and is used as a flavouring.

Effects on Health A question mark as to its safety hangs over this additive. There has been a reduction in the number of kinds available to the food industry. Work is in hand to discover the safest form. One kind which is produced with ammonia has been shown to cause vitamin B6 deficiency in rats.

Flavouring

Effects on Health Debatable, as no information is available. Many substances in this category are artificially synthesised; safety cannot be assumed.

E338 Phosphoric Acid Has a synergist effect, enhances the antioxidant effect of other substances; used as a flavouring.
Effects on Health No known health risk in food.

E211 Sodium Benzoate

Preserves, is antibacterial and antifungal.
Effects on Health People who are prone to skin rashes or are asthmatic may have allergic reactions. This additive is one that is recommended by the Hyperactive Children's Support Group to be avoided by food-sensitive children and adults who are aspirin sensitive.

also

TESCO COLA

SAFEWAY COLA

Cooked Ham Tinned

SAINSBURY'S COOKED HAM

Sugar**   *Salt***

E450(c) Sodium Polyphosphates Emulsifying salts; used to stabilise.
Effects on Health French research suggests that polyphosphates might block a number of enzymes, causing digestive disturbances.

E250 Sodium Nitrite Preserves food and inhibits the growth of the bacterium responsible for botulism.

Effects on Health Nitrites may interact with amines from foods in the stomach to form nitrosamines which are known to cause cancer in animals. They are also taboo in foods for babies and young children. Such an additive can cause allergic reactions and is on the list of foods not recommended by the Hyperactive Children's Support Group.

also

PRINCES COOKED HAM

E301 Sodium L-ascorbate
Provides vitamin C and is used as an antioxidant and to preserve colour.
Effects on Health There is no health risk.

OAK HAM
Sugar**   *Salt***

E450(a) Tetrasodium Diphosphate Used to emulsify.
Effects on Health No health risk known.

621 Monosodium Glutamate
Enhances the flavour of foods containing protein by stimulating the taste buds or increasing the degree of saliva produced in the mouth.
Effects on Health Responsible for symptoms of palpitation, headache, dizziness, nausea, muscle tightness, a feeling of weakness in the forearms, pains in the neck, and other, migraine-like symptoms in some people. This substance is recommended to be excluded from the diets of hyperactive children; it is also taboo in or on food intended for babies and young children.

E301 Sodium L-ascorbate
Provides vitamin C and is used as an antioxidant and to preserve colour.
Effects on Health There is no health risk.

E250 Sodium Nitrite Preserves food and inhibits the growth of the bacterium responsible for botulism.
Effects on Health Nitrites may interact with amines from foods in the stomach to form nitrosamines which are known to cause cancer in animals. They are also taboo in foods for babies and young children. Such an additive can cause allergic reactions and is on the list of foods not recommended by the Hyperactive Children's Support Group.

also

TUDOR QUEEN HAM

SMC HAM

HAMBURG HOLLAND HAM
Sugar**   *Salt***

E450(a) Tetrasodium Diphosphate Used to emulsify.
Effects on Health No health risk known.

E450(b) Pentasodium Triphosphate Used to provide texture and is an emulsifying salt.
Effects on Health French research suggests that polyphosphates can block a number of enzymes, causing digestive disturbances.

E450(c) Sodium Polyphosphates Emulsifying salts; used to stabilise.

Effects on Health French research suggests that polyphosphates might block a number of enzymes, causing digestive disturbances.

E301 Sodium L-ascorbate
Provides vitamin C and is used as an antioxidant and to preserve colour.
Effects on Health There is no health risk.

621 Monosodium Glutamate
Enhances the flavour of foods containing protein by stimulating the taste buds or increasing the degree of saliva produced in the mouth.
Effects on Health Responsible for symptoms of palpitation, headache, dizziness, nausea, muscle tightness, a feeling of weakness in the forearms, pains in the neck, and other,

migraine-like symptoms in some people. This substance is recommended to be excluded from the diets of hyperactive children; it is also taboo in or on food intended for babies and young children.

E250 Sodium Nitrite Preserves food and inhibits the growth of the bacterium responsible for botulism.
Effects on Health Nitrites may interact with amines from foods in the stomach to form nitrosamines which are known to cause cancer in animals. They are also taboo in foods for babies and young children. Such an additive can cause allergic reactions and is on the list of foods not recommended by the Hyperactive Children's Support Group.

Cottage Cheese

MATTESSONS

E415 Corn Sugar Gum Used to stabilise and thicken.
Effects on Health There are no known health risks.

E412 Guar Gum Used to thicken; a bulking agent.
Effects on Health Harmless except when consumed to excess when nausea, flatulence and stomach cramps might occur.

CO-OP
Sugar   Salt**

E412 Guar Gum Used to thicken; a bulking agent.
Effects on Health Harmless except when consumed to excess when nausea, flatulence and stomach cramps might occur.

E415 Corn Sugar Gum Used to stabilise and thicken.
Effects on Health There are no known health risks.

E410 Locust Bean Gum
Stabilises, emulsifies; a gelling agent.
Effects on Health No known health risks. The pods of the bean have been eaten since Biblical times. The refined gum could cause stomach pain and swelling if eaten in quantity.

E202 Potassium Sorbate A preservative that is antifungal and antibacterial.

Effects on Health Not known as a health risk.

also

SAFEWAY

ST IVEL

EDEN VALE

Creamed Rice Pudding

LIBBYS CREAMED RICE PUDDING

*Sugar***   *Salt*

No additives

SAINSBURY'S CREAMED RICE PUDDING

*Sugar***   *Salt*

500 Sodium Bicarbonate
Used to balance alkaline/acid levels and to aerate.
Effects on Health Not known as a health risk.

also

CO-OP CREAMED RICE PUDDING

FINE FARE YELLOW PACK

*Sugar***   *Salt*

E331 Sodium Citrates Acts as a synergist, i.e. enhances the effects of other antioxidants; an emulsifying salt and controls the acid/alkaline level.
Effects on Health No known health risk.

E160(a) Alpha-carotene, Beta-carotene, Gamma-carotene Gives a yellow-orange colour to product, converts to vitamin A in the body.
Effects on Health There are no known health risks.

also

TESCO VALUE PACK

SAFEWAY TRADITIONAL STYLE CREAMED RICE PUDDING

Sugar**   *Salt*

E339(b) Disodium Hydrogen Orthophosphate A gelling agent and stabiliser, maintains acidity/alkalinity at a determined level.
Effects on Health No health risks known.

E331 Sodium Citrates Acts as a synergist, i.e. enhances the effects of other antioxidants; an emulsifying salt and controls the acid/alkaline level.
Effects on Health No known health risks.

E160(a) Alpha-carotene, Beta-carotene, Gamma-carotene Gives a yellow-orange colour to product, converts to vitamin A in the body.
Effects on Health Not known as a health risk.

Custard Creams and Cream Biscuits

McVITIE'S NATURAL CHOICE YOGHOURT CREAMS

Sugar***   *Salt**

500 Sodium Bicarbonate
Used to balance alkaline/acid levels and to aerate.
Effects on Health Not known as a health risk.

503 Ammonium Carbonate
Used to maintain the alkaline/acid pH at a determined level; to aerate.
Effects on Health Not known as a health risk.

SAINSBURY'S CUSTARD CREAMS

Sugar**   *Salt***

Modified Starch Used as thickener. An umbrella term for 18 substances not defined by 'E' numbers.
Effects on Health No suggestion that they are harmful.

Flavourings
Effects on Health Debatable, as no information is available. Many substances in this category are artificially synthesised; safety cannot be assumed.

E160(b) Annatto Bixin Norbixin Gives a yellow to

peach colour to product.
Effects on Health Safe except for reports of hives in some people.

CO-OP CUSTARD CREAMS

Sugar***   *Salt***

Flavourings
Effects on Health Debatable, as no information is available. Many substances in this category are artificially synthesised; safety cannot be assumed.

E322 Lecithin Acts as an emulsifier and stabiliser; it is an antioxidant and gives additional thickness to fats.
Effects on Health There are no known health risks; in fact, lecithin is used therapeutically to mobilise fats in the body and has also been experimented with in the treatment of senile dementia.

E102 Tartrazine Gives yellow colour to product.
Effects on Health Has been implicated with causing sleeplessness at night in hyperactive and food-sensitive children. Symptoms including skin rashes, hay fever, problems with breathing, blurred vision and purple skin patches are reported in susceptible people, particularly those who are aspirin sensitive or asthmatic.

E110 Sunset Yellow FCF Gives yellow colour to product.

Effects on Health One of the azo-dye family which is recommended to be excluded from the diets of hyperactive children. Adults may have an allergic reaction with symptoms of skin rash, swollen blood vessels and gastric problems, especially if aspirin sensitive.

TESCO CUSTARD CREAMS

Sugar**   *Salt**

E320 Butylated Hydroxyanisole As an antioxidant this works alone or in conjunction with a synergist, i.e. citric acid or phosphoric acid, which enhances its effect. It prevents rancidity and also delays flavour deterioration due to oxidation.
Effects on Health It raises the lipid and cholesterol levels in the blood. Because it encourages the formation of metabolising enzymes in the liver there is the increased risk of breakdown of important substances in the body such as vitamin D. The Hyperactive Children's Support Group recommend that this is not included in the diet of food-sensitive children. It is not permitted in foods intended for babies and young children with the exception of its use to preserve added vitamin A.

Flavourings
Effects on Health Debatable, as no information is available. Many substances in this

category are artificially synthesised; safety cannot be assumed.

E322 Lecithin Acts as an emulsifier and stabiliser; it is an antioxidant and gives additional thickness to fats.
Effects on Health There are no known health risks; in fact, lecithin is used therapeutically to mobilise fats in the body and has also been experimented with in the treatment of senile dementia.

E160(a) Alpha-carotene, Beta-carotene, Gamma-carotene
Colours food orange-yellow; converts to vitamin A in the body.
Effects on Health No known health risks.

503 Ammonium Carbonate
Used to maintain alkaline/acid pH at a determined level and to aerate.
Effects on Health Not known as a health risk.

Custard Powder

TESCO
Sugar   Salt**

Flavouring
Effects on Health Debatable, as no information is available. Many substances in this category are artificially synthesised; safety cannot be assumed.

E102 Tartrazine Gives yellow colouring to product.
Effects on Health Has been implicated with causing sleeplessness at night in hyperactive and food-sensitive children. Symptoms including skin rash, hay fever, problems with breathing, blurred vision and purple skin patches are reported in susceptible people, particularly those who are aspirin sensitive or asthmatic.

E110 Sunset Yellow FCF
Gives yellow colouring to product.
Effects on Health One of the azo-dye family which is recommended to be excluded from the diets of hyperactive children. Adults may have an allergic reaction with symptoms of skin rash, swollen blood vessels and gastric problems, especially if aspirin sensitive.

also

WAITROSE

SAFEWAY

FINE FARE

SAINSBURY'S INSTANT CUSTARD MIX
*Sugar*** *Salt***

E471 Mono- and Di-glycerides of Fatty Acids
Used to emulsify and stabilise.
Effects on Health Not known as a health risk.

E102 Tartrazine Gives yellow colouring to product.
Effects on Health Has been implicated with causing sleeplessness at night in hyperactive and food-sensitive children. Symptoms including skin rash, hay fever, problems with breathing, blurred vision and purple skin patches are reported in susceptible people, particularly those who are aspirin sensitive or asthmatic.

E110 Sunset Yellow FCF
Gives yellow colouring to product.
Effects on Health One of the azo-dye family which is recommended to be excluded from the diets of hyperactive children. Adults may have an allergic reaction with symptoms of skin rash, swollen blood vessels and gastric problems, especially if aspirin sensitive.

E127 Erythrosine Gives red colouring to product. A coal-tar dye.
Effects on Health This additive can cause sensitivity to light and has also been recommended by the Hyperactive Children's Support Group to be excluded from the diets of hyperactive children. Because it contains 577mg of iodine per gram there is a risk that the consuming of a number of foods which contain E127 might cause an overactive thyroid.

Flavourings
Effects on Health Debatable, as no information is available. Many substances in this category are artificially synthesised; safety cannot be assumed.

also

BIRD'S WHISK AND SERVE

BROWN AND POLSON'S
*Sugar*** *Salt*

Modified Starch Used as thickener. An umbrella term for 18 substances not defined by 'E' numbers.
Effects on Health No suggestion that they are harmful.

E450(b) Pentasodium Triphosphate Used to provide texture and is an emulsifying salt.
Effects on Health French research suggests that polyphosphates can block a number of enzymes, causing digestive disturbances.

Flavourings
Effects on Health Debatable, as no information is available. Many substances in this category are artificially synthesised; safety cannot be assumed.

E340(a) Potassium Dihydrogen Orthophosphate

Used to maintain alkalinity/acidity at a determined level; an emulsifying salt, enhances the action of other antioxidants.
Effects on Health No known health risk.

E471 Mono- and Di-glycerides of Fatty Acids

Used to emulsify and stabilise.
Effects on Health No known health risks.

E472(b) Lactic Esters of Mono- and Di-glycerides of Fatty Acids

Emulsifies and stabilises.
Effects on Health Not known as a health risk

E102 Tartrazine

Gives yellow colouring to product.
Effects on Health Has been implicated with causing sleeplessness at night in hyperactive and food-sensitive children. Symptoms including skin rashes, hay fever, problems with breathing, blurred vision and purple skin patches are reported in susceptible people, particularly those who are aspirin sensitive or asthmatic.

E110 Sunset Yellow FCF

Gives yellow colouring to product.
Effects on Health One of the azo-dye family which is recommended to be excluded from the diets of hyperactive children. Adults may have an allergic reaction with symptoms of skin rash, swollen blood vessels and gastric problems, especially if aspirin sensitive.

E124 Ponceau 4R

Gives red colouring to product.
Effects on Health One of the azo-dye family which is recommended to be excluded from the diets of hyperactive children. Adults who are aspirin sensitive may be affected.

CO-OP INSTANT CUSTARD POWDER

Sugar***   *Salt***

E415 Corn Sugar Gum

Used to stabilise or thicken.
Effects on Health There are no health risks known.

E340 Potassium Dihydrogen Orthophosphate

Used to maintain alkalinity/acidity at a determined level; an emulsifying salt, enhances the action of other antioxidants.
Effects on Health No known health risk.

Flavouring

Effects on Health Debatable, as no information is available. Many substances in this category are artificially synthesised; safety cannot be assumed.

E110 Sunset Yellow FCF

Gives yellow colouring to product.
Effects on Health One of the azo-dye family which is recommended to be excluded

from the diets of hyperactive children. Adults may have an allergic reaction with symptoms of skin rash, swollen blood vessels and gastric problems, especially if aspirin sensitive.

E122 Carmoisine Gives red colouring to product.
Effects on Health This has been recommended by the Hyperactive Children's Support Group as unsuitable for children who are food sensitive. An azo-dye, it may produce adverse

reactions in those people who have an aspirin allergy or are asthmatic. Such reactions can include skin rashes or swelling.

E124 Ponceau 4R Gives red colouring to product.
Effects on Health One of the azo-dye family which is recommended to be excluded from the diets of hyperactive children. Adults who are aspirin sensitive or asthmatic may be affected.

Dessert Syrups and Sauces

TESCO
Sugar***   *Salt*

No additives

WALLS CHOCOLATE DESSERT SAUCE
Sugar***   *Salt*

E216 Propyl 4-Hydroxybenzoate It is antibacterial and used as a preservative.
Effects on Health This additive can be added to the Hyperactive Children's Support Group list of substances not recommended to be given to food-sensitive children; it may also be dangerous to asthmatics or those who have aspirin sensitivity.

ASKEY'S CHOCOLATE DESSERT SYRUP
Sugar**   *Salt*

E330 Citric Acid Stabilises the acidity of food substances, prevents discoloration of fruit, keeps the flavour 'true' and retains vitamin C.
Effects on Health Needs to be consumed in very large quantities to erode teeth or irritate locally.

E123 Amaranth Gives red colour to product.
Effects on Health As an azo-dye it should be avoided by people who are sensitive to aspirin as it may cause a skin rash. The Hyperactive Children's Support Group recommend it is excluded from the diets of food-sensitive children.

E142 Acid Brilliant Green
Gives green colour to product.
Effects on Health No ill effects
reported although as a synthetic
dye it may affect hyperactive
children and those who suffer
from asthma or are aspirin
sensitive.

E155 Brown HT Gives brown
colour to product.
Effects on Health As an azo-dye
this should be avoided by
people who are asthmatic or
have aspirin sensitivity. It is also
recommended by the
Hyperactive Children's Support
Group to be avoided by
children who are food sensitive.

E220 Sulphur Dioxide
Preserves and acts as an
antioxidant or improving agent;
stabilises vitamin C.
Effects on Health Irritates the
alimentary food canal; destroys
much of flour's vitamin E
content. It is one of the
additives which the Hyperactive
Children's Support Group
recommend be avoided by food-
sensitive children.

BIRD'S ICE MAGIC
Sugar**   *Salt*

**E320 Butylated
Hydroxyanisole** As an
antioxidant this works alone or
in conjunction with a synergist,
i.e. citric acid or phosphoric
acid, which enhances its effect.
It prevents rancidity and also

delays flavour deterioration due
to oxidation.
Effects on Health It raises the
lipid and cholesterol levels in
the blood. Because it encourages
the formation of metabolising
enzymes in the liver there is the
increased risk of breakdown of
important substances in the
body such as vitamin D. The
Hyperactive Children's Support
Group recommend that this is
not included in the diet of food-
sensitive children. It is not
permitted in foods intended for
babies and young children with
the exception of its use to preserve
added vitamin A.

E310 Propyl Gallate Used as
an antioxidant in fats and oils.
Effects on Health These members
of the alkyl gallate group are
capable of causing gastric
irritation and problems for
people who are sensitive to
aspirin or suffer from asthma. A
report exists implying that
propyl gallate could cause liver
damage and reproductive
failure. The additive is taboo in
foods intended for babies and
young children. It can be added
to the list of foods not recommended by the Hyperactive
Children's Support Group.

E330 Citric Acid Stabilises the
acidity of food substances,
prevents discoloration of fruit,
keeps the flavour 'true' and
retains vitamin C.
Effects on Health Needs to be
consumed in very large
quantities to erode teeth or
irritate locally.

Dessert Toppings

NESTLÉ'S TIP TOP
Sugar**   *Salt**

Modified Starch Used as thickener. An umbrella term for 18 substances not defined by 'E' numbers.
Effects on Health No suggestion that they are harmful.

'Emulsifiers', which must be specified from January 1986.
Effects on Health No health risks are likely.

Flavourings
Effects on Health Debatable, as no information is available. Many substances in this category are artificially synthesised; safety cannot be assumed.

CO-OP INSTANT DESSERT TOPPING
Sugar***   *Salt*

Modified Starch Used as thickener. An umbrella term for 18 substances not defined by 'E' numbers.
Effects on Health No suggestion that they are harmful.

E477 Propane-1, 2-Diol Esters of Fatty Acids Used to emulsify or stabilise.
Effects on Health No known health risk.

Flavourings
Effects on Health Debatable, as no information is available. Many substances in this category are artificially synthesised; safety cannot be assumed.

E110 Sunset Yellow FCF Gives yellow colouring to product.
Effects on Health One of the azo-dye family which is recommended to be excluded from the diets of hyperactive children. Adults may have an allergic reaction with symptoms of skin rash, swollen blood vessels and gastric problems, especially if aspirin sensitive.

E102 Tartrazine Gives yellow colouring to product.
Effects on Health Has been implicated with causing sleeplessness at night in hyperactive and food-sensitive children. Symptoms including skin rash, hay fever, problems with breathing, blurred vision and purple skin patches are reported in susceptible people, particularly those who are aspirin sensitive or asthmatic.

SAINSBURY'S TOPPING

*Sugar**   Salt*

E477 Propane-1, 2-Diol Esters of Fatty Acids Used to emulsify and stabilise.
Effects on Health No known health risk.

E322 Lecithin Acts as an emulsifier and stabiliser; it is an antioxidant and gives additional thickness to fats.
Effects on Health There are no known health risks; in fact, lecithin is used therapeutically to mobilise fats in the body and has also been experimented with in the treatment of senile dementia.

Modified Starch Used as thickener. An umbrella term for 18 substances not defined by 'E' numbers.
Effects on Health No suggestion that they are harmful.

Flavouring
Effects on Health Debatable, as no information is available. Many substances in this category are artificially synthesised; safety cannot be assumed.

E320 Butylated Hydroxyanisole As an antioxidant this works alone or in conjunction with a synergist, i.e. citric acid or phosphoric acid, which enhances its effect. It prevents rancidity and also delays flavour deterioration due to oxidation.
Effects on Health It raises the lipid and cholesterol levels in the blood. Because it encourages the formation of metabolising enzymes in the liver there is the increased risk of breakdown of important substances in the body such as vitamin D. The Hyperactive Children's Support Group recommend that this is not included in the diet of food-sensitive children. It is not permitted in foods intended for babies and young children with the exception of its use to preserve added vitamin A.

E160(a) Alpha-carotene, Beta-carotene, Gamma-carotene Gives a yellow-orange colour to product.
Effects on Health No health risks known.

also

BIRD'S DREAM TOPPING

Dried Skimmed Milk

ST IVEL 'FIVE PINTS'

*Sugar*** *Salt*

E471 Mono- and Di-glycerides of Fatty Acids An emulsifier and stabiliser.
Effects on Health Not known as a health risk.

551 Silica Used to prevent particles sticking together; to thicken and stabilise.
Effects on Health No ill effects known.

E322 Lecithin Acts as an emulsifier and stabiliser; it is an antioxidant and gives additional thickness to fats.
Effects on Health There are no known health risks; in fact, lecithin is used therapeutically to mobilise fats in the body and has also been experimented with in the treatment of senile dementia.

SAINSBURY'S 'EASY PINTS'

*Sugar**** *Salt*

E322 Lecithin Acts as an emulsifier and stabiliser; it is an antioxidant and gives additional thickness to fats.
Effects on Health There are no

known health risks; in fact, lecithin is used therapeutically to mobilise fats in the body and has also been experimented with in the treatment of senile dementia.

554 Aluminium Sodium Silicate Used to prevent particles sticking together.
Effects on Health Some people react to aluminium and others should avoid excess salt; so not entirely free of health risks.

E160(a) Annatto Bixin Norbixin Gives a yellow to peach colour to product.
Effects on Health Safe except for reports of hives in some people.

also

CO-OP DRIED SKIMMED MILK

SAFEWAY 'FAST PINTS'

*Sugar**** *Salt*

E322 Lecithin Acts as an emulsifier and stabiliser; it is an antioxidant and gives additional thickness to fats.
Effects on Health There are no known health risks; in fact, lecithin is used therapeutically

to mobilise fats in the body and has also been experimented with in the treatment of senile dementia.

E471 Mono- and Di- glycerides of Fatty Acids An emulsifier and stabiliser.
Effects on Health Not known as a health risk.

554 Aluminium Sodium Silicate Used to prevent particles sticking together.
Effects on Health Some people react to aluminium and others should avoid excess salt; so not entirely free of health risk.

E160(a) Annatto Bixin Norbixin Gives a yellow to peach colour to product.
Effects on Health Safe except for reports of hives in some people.

KERRYGOLD 'PLENTY'
Sugar**   *Salt*

E320 Butylated Hydroxyanisole As an antioxidant this works alone or in conjunction with a synergist, i.e. citric acid or phosphoric acid, which enhances its effect. It prevents rancidity and also delays flavour deterioration due to oxidation.
Effects on Health It raises the lipid and cholesterol levels in the blood. Because it encourages the formation of metabolising enzymes in the liver there is the

increased risk of breakdown of important substances in the body such as vitamin D. The Hyperactive Children's Support Group recommend that this is not included in the diet of food-sensitive children. It is not permitted in foods intended for babies and young children with the exception of its use to preserve added vitamin A.

E471 Mono- and Di- glycerides of Fatty Acids An emulsifier and stabiliser.
Effects on Health Not known as a health risk.

E322 Lecithin Acts as an emulsifier and stabiliser; it is an antioxidant and gives additional thickness to fats.
Effects on Health There are no known health risks; in fact, lecithin is used therapeutically to mobilise fats in the body and has also been experimented with in the treatment of senile dementia.

554 Aluminium Sodium Silicate Used to prevent particles sticking together.
Effects on Health Some people react to aluminium, others should avoid excessive sodium; so not entirely free of health risk.

E160(a) Annatto Bixin Norbixin Gives a yellow to peach colour to product.
Effects on Health Safe except for reports of hives in some people.

Fish Fingers

WAITROSE FISH FINGERS
Sugar   Salt**

No additives

ROSS JUMBO FISH FINGERS
Sugar   Salt**

Modified Starch Used as thickener. An umbrella term for 18 substances not defined by 'E' numbers.
Effects on Health No suggestion that they are harmful.

E450(a) Tetrasodium Diphosphate Maintains acidity/alkalinity at a determined level; an emulsifying salt and stabiliser, also gelling agent.
Effects on Health No health risks known.

500(11) Sodium Sesquicarbonate Used to increase alkalinity or decrease acidity.
Effects on Health There are no known health risks.

E450(c) Sodium Polyphosphates Emulsifying salt used to stabilise.

Effects on Health French research suggests that polyphosphates might block a number of enzymes, causing digestive disturbances.

TESCO FISH FINGERS
Sugar   Salt**

E102 Tartrazine Gives yellow colouring to product.
Effects on Health Has been implicated with causing sleeplessness at night in hyperactive and food-sensitive children. Symptoms including skin rash, hay fever, problems with breathing, blurred vision and purple skin patches are reported in susceptible people, particularly those who are aspirin sensitive or asthmatic.

E124 Ponceau 4R Gives red colouring to product.
Effects on Health One of the azo-dye family which is recommended to be excluded from the diets of hyperactive children. Adults who are aspirin sensitive or asthmatic may be affected.

Plus (for Co-op and Safeway):
E450(c) Sodium Polyphosphates Emulsifying salts used to stabilise.

Effects on Health French research suggests that polyphosphates might block a number of enzymes, causing digestive disturbances.

also

GATEWAY FISH FINGERS

CO-OP FISH FINGERS

SAFEWAY FISH FINGERS

FINE FARE YELLOW PACK

Sugar   Salt**

E450(c) Sodium Polyphosphates Emulsifying salts used to stabilise.
Effects on Health French research suggests that polyphosphates might block a number of enzymes, causing digestive disturbances.

621 Monosodium Glutamate Enhances the flavour of foods containing protein by stimulating the taste buds or increasing the degree of saliva produced in the mouth.
Effects on Health Responsible for symptoms of palpitation, headache, dizziness, nausea, muscle tightness, a feeling of weakness in the forearms, pains in the neck, and other,

migraine-like symptoms in some people. This substance is recommended by the Hyperactive Children's Support Group to be excluded from the diets of hyperactive children; it is also taboo in or on food intended for babies and young children.

E102 Tartrazine Gives yellow colouring to product.
Effects on Health Has been implicated with causing sleeplessness at night in hyperactive and food-sensitive children. Symptoms including skin rashes, hay fever, problems with breathing, blurred vision and purple skin patches are reported in susceptible people, particularly those who are aspirin sensitive or asthmatic.

E124 Ponceau 4R Gives red colouring to product.
Effects on Health One of the azo-dye family which is recommended to be excluded from the diets of hyperactive children. Adults who are aspirin sensitive or asthmatic may be affected adversely.

E110 Sunset Yellow FCF Gives yellow colouring to product.
Effects on Health One of the azo-dye family which is recommended to be excluded from the diets of hyperactive children. Adults may have an allergic reaction with symptoms of skin rash, swollen blood vessels and gastric problems, especially if aspirin sensitive.

Fruit Cake

YORKSHIRE FARM BAKERY

Sugar**   *Salt**

No added preservatives or colours

HALES GRANNIES' FRUIT CAKE

Sugar**   *Salt***

No added preservatives or colours

SAFEWAY ALL BUTTER WHEATMEAL FRUIT CAKE

Sugar***   *Salt***

E420(11) Sorbitol Syrup Used for sweetening and also to prevent products from drying out.
Effects on Health When taken in excess it can cause flatulence, diarrhoea and distension of stomach. It is however of use to diabetics as it does not raise the blood sugar level significantly and is well tolerated.

McVITIE'S KENSINGTON CAKE

Sugar**   *Salt***

E420(11) Sorbitol Syrup Used for sweetening and also to prevent products from drying out.
Effects on Health When taken in excess it can cause flatulence, diarrhoea and distension of stomach. It is however of use to diabetics as it does not raise the blood sugar level significantly and is well tolerated.

500 Sodium Bicarbonate Used to balance alkaline/acid levels and to aerate.
Effects on Health Not known as a health risk.

E450(a) Tetrasodium Diphosphate Maintains pH at a determined acid/alkaline level; emulsifies, stabilises or is a gelling agent.
Effects on Health Not known as a health risk.

Flavourings
Effects on Health Debatable, as no information is available. Many substances in this category are artificially synthesised; safety cannot be assumed.

E102 Tartrazine Gives yellow colouring to product.

Effects on Health Has been implicated with causing sleeplessness at night in hyperactive and food-sensitive children. Symptoms including skin rash, hay fever, problems with breathing, blurred vision and purple skin patches are reported in susceptible people, particularly those who are aspirin sensitive or asthmatic.

E110 Sunset Yellow FCF
Gives yellow colouring to product.
Effects on Health One of the azo-dye family which is recommended to be excluded from the diets of hyperactive children. Adults may have an allergic reaction with symptoms of skin rash, swollen blood vessels and gastric problems, especially if aspirin sensitive.

E471 Mono- and Di-glycerides of Fatty Acids
An emulsifier and stabiliser.
Effects on Health Not known as a health risk.

SAINSBURY'S FRUIT CAKE
Sugar***   Salt**

E471 Mono- and Di-glycerides of Fatty Acids
An emulsifier and stabiliser.
Effects on Health Not known as a health risk.

E330 Citric Acid Stabilises the acidity of food substances, prevents discoloration of fruit, keeps the flavour 'true' and

retains vitamin C.
Effects on Health Needs to be consumed in very large quantities to erode teeth or irritate locally.

E102 Tartrazine Gives yellow colouring to product.
Effects on Health Has been implicated with causing sleeplessness at night in hyperactive and food-sensitive children. Symptoms including skin rash, hay fever, problems with breathing, blurred vision and purple skin patches are reported in susceptible people, particularly those who are aspirin sensitive or asthmatic.

E110 Sunset Yellow FCF
Gives yellow colouring to product.
Effects on Health One of the azo-dye family which is recommended to be excluded from the diets of hyperactive children. Adults may have an allergic reaction with symptoms of skin rash, swollen blood vessels and gastric problems, especially if aspirin sensitive.

E142 Acid Brilliant Green
Gives green colouring to product.
Effects on Health No ill effects are reported although, as a synthetic dye, it may affect hyperactive children and those who suffer from asthma or are aspirin sensitive.

E150 Caramel Gives brown colouring to product and is used as a flavouring.
Effects on Health A question mark hangs over this additive as to its safety. There has been a

reduction in the number of kinds available to the food industry. Work is in hand to discover the safest form. One kind which is produced with ammonia has been shown to cause vitamin B6 deficiency in rats.

Flavouring
Effects on Health Debatable, as no information is available.

Many substances in this category are artificially synthesised; safety cannot be assumed.

E200 Sorbic Acid Used to preserve, and to inhibit the growth of moulds and yeasts.
Effects on Health There is a possibility of irritation of skin.

Fruit Filling for Pies

SAINSBURY'S APPLE FILLING
Sugar** Salt

Modified Starch Used as thickener. An umbrella term for 18 substances not defined by 'E' numbers.
Effects on Health No suggestion that they are harmful.

E330 Citric Acid Stabilises the acidity of food substances, prevents discoloration of fruit, keeps the flavour 'true' and retains vitamin C.
Effects on Health Needs to be consumed in very large quantities to erode teeth or irritate locally.

also

PICKERINGS REAL FRUIT PIE FILLING
Sugar*** Salt

CO-OP APPLE FRUIT FILLING

BATCHELORS PACK-A-PIE FILLING
Sugar*** Salt

Modified Starch Used as thickener. An umbrella term for 18 substances not defined by 'E' numbers.
Effects on Health No suggestion that they are harmful.

E331 Sodium Citrates Acts as a synergist, i.e. enhances the effects of other antioxidants, and an emulsifying salt, and controls the acid/alkaline level.
Effects on Health No known health risk.

E330 Citric Acid Stabilises the acidity of food substances, prevents discoloration of fruit, keeps the flavour 'true' and retains vitamin C.
Effects on Health Needs to be consumed in very large quantities to erode teeth or irritate locally.

E401 Sodium Alginate
Stabilises, thickens and
emulsifies.
Effects on Health No known
health risks.

**E341(a) Calcium
Tetrahydrogen
Diorthophosphate** Used to
maintain alkalinity/acidity at a
determined level, and to prevent
softening of fruit during
processing; an emulsifying salt
and raising agent, enhances
action of other antioxidants.

Effects on Health No known
health risks.

E202 Potassium Sorbate A
preservative that is antifungal
and antibacterial.
Effects on Health No known
health risks.

E171 Titanium Dioxide Gives
a white colouring to the surface
of a product.
Effects on Health No known
health risks.

Glacé Cherries

SAINSBURY'S GLACÉ CHERRIES
Sugar**   *Salt*

E127 Erythrosine Gives red
colouring to product. A coal-tar
dye.
Effects on Health Can cause light
sensitivity. It is recommended
by the Hyperactive Children's
Support Group to be excluded
from the diets of food-sensitive
children. Because it contains
577mg of iodine per gram there
is a risk, if the consumption of
E127 additives is in excess, of
problems with an over-active
thyroid.

E200 Sorbic Acid A
preservative which inhibits the
growth of yeasts and moulds.
Effects on Health Possibility of
skin irritation.

CO-OP GLACÉ CHERRIES
Sugar***   *Salt*

E202 Potassium Sorbate A
preservative which is antifungal
and antibacterial.
Effects on Health No risks to
health known.

E220 Sulphur Dioxide
Preserves, is an antioxidant and
improving agent; stabilises
vitamin C.
Effects on Health There is a
possibility of irritation of the
food canal. Destroys much of
flour's vitamin E during
bleaching. Is one of the
additives recommended by the
Hyperactive Children's Support
Group to be excluded from the
diets of food-sensitive children.

E127 Erythrosine Gives red colouring to product. A coal-tar dye.
Effects on Health Can cause sensitivity to light. It is recommended by the Hyperactive Children's Support Group to be excluded from the diets of food-sensitive children. Because it contains 577mg of iodine per gram there is a risk, if the consumption of E127 additives is in excess, of problems with an over-active thyroid.

also

FINE FARE

GATEWAY

SAFEWAY

Gravy Granules

SAINSBURY'S GRAVY GRANULES
*Sugar   Salt****

Modified Starch Used as thickener. An umbrella term for 18 substances not defined by 'E' numbers.
Effects on Health No suggestion that they are harmful.

E150 Caramel Gives brown colour to product and is used as a flavouring.
Effects on Health A question mark as to its safety hangs over this additive. There has been a reduction in the number of kinds available to the food industry. Work is in hand to discover the safest form. One type which is produced with ammonia has been shown to cause vitamin B6 deficiency in rats.

E472(e) Mono- and Diacetyltartaric Acid Esters of Mono- and Di-Glycerides of Fatty Acids Emulsifies and stabilises.
Effects on Health No known health risk.

E482 Calcium Stearoyl-2-Lactylate Emulsifies and stabilises; an aid to whipping.
Effects on Health No known health risk.

554 Aluminium Sodium Silicate Prevents particles sticking together.
Effects on Health Some people react to aluminium, others should avoid excess sodium; so not entirely free of health risk.

621 Monosodium Glutamate Enhances the flavour of foods containing protein by stimulating the taste buds or increasing the degree of saliva produced in the mouth.
Effects on Health Responsible for

such symptoms as palpitation, headache, dizziness, nausea, muscle tightness, a feeling of weakness in the forearms, pains in the neck, and other, migraine-like symptoms in some people. This substance is recommended to be excluded from the diets of hyperactive children; it is also taboo in or on foods intended for babies and young children.

631 Sodium Inosinate
Enhances flavour.
Effects on Health This is taboo in or on foods made specially for babies and young children. It should be avoided by people who suffer from gout and related problems requiring the avoidance of purines. It is also recommended to be excluded from the diets of hyperactive children by the Hyperactive Children's Support Group. It can cause problems for asthmatics or those who are aspirin sensitive.

627 Guanosine 5′ Enhances
flavour.
Effects on Health This is taboo in or on foods made specially for babies and young children. It should be avoided by people who suffer from gout and related problems requiring the avoidance of purines. It is also recommended to be excluded from the diets of hyperactive children by the Hyperactive Children's Support Group. It can cause problems for asthmatics or those who are aspirin sensitive.

E320 Butylated Hydroxyanisole As an
antioxidant this works alone or in conjunction with a synergist, i.e. citric acid or phosphoric acid, which enhances its effect. It prevents rancidity and also delays flavour deterioration due to oxidation.
Effects on Health It raises the lipid and cholesterol levels in the blood. Because it encourages the formation of metabolising enzymes in the liver there is the increased risk of breakdown of important substances in the body such as vitamin D. The Hyperactive Children's Support Group recommend that this is not included in the diet of food-sensitive children. It is not permitted in foods intended for babies and young children with the exception of its use to preserve added vitamin A.

E321 Butylated Hydroxytoluene Used as an
antioxidant for food fats and oils.
Effects on Health Those who are sensitive to this antioxidant may develop rashes. It can increase the rate of breakdown of other substances in the body, i.e. vitamin D, because of the development of metabolising enzymes. Other reports link this additive with a possibility of reproductive failures, blood cell changes and effects on behaviour. The Hyperactive Children's Support Group include this on the list of substances not recommended for food-sensitive children, and it is

taboo in foods intended for babies and young children with the exception of its use to preserve added vitamin A. There have been conflicting research reports on its effect on rats.

Plus (for Waitrose and Bisto):

Flavourings
Effects on Health Debatable, as no information is available. Many substances in this category are artificially synthesised; safety cannot be assumed.

also

WAITROSE GRAVY GRANULES

BISTO RICH GRAVY GRANULES

CO-OP'S GRAVY GRANULES

*Sugar   Salt****

Modified Starch Used as thickener. An umbrella term for 18 substances not defined by 'E' numbers.
Effects on Health No suggestion that they are harmful.

E150 Caramel Gives brown colouring to product and is used as a flavouring.
Effects on Health A question mark as to its safety hangs over

this additive. There has been a reduction in the number of kinds available to the food industry. Work is in hand to discover the safest form. One type which is produced with ammonia has been shown to cause vitamin B6 deficiency in rats.

E102 Tartrazine Gives yellow colour to product.
Effects on Health Has been implicated with causing sleeplessness at night in hyperactive and food-sensitive children. Symptoms including skin rashes, hay fever, problems with breathing, blurred vision and purple skin patches are reported in susceptible people, particularly those who are aspirin sensitive or asthmatic.

E122 Carmoisine Gives red colour to product.
Effects on Health This has been recommended by the Hyperactive Children's Support Group as unsuitable for children who are food sensitive. An azo-dye, it may produce adverse reactions in people who have an aspirin allergy or are asthmatic. Such reactions can include skin rashes or swelling.

E151 Black PN Gives black colour to product.
Effects on Health Further research into the effects of this additive is needed. One 90-day feeding study on pigs revealed the presence of intestinal cysts. This features on the list of additives which the Hyperactive Children's Support

Group do not recommend be given to hyperactive children.

E142 Acid Brilliant Green

Gives green colour to product.
Effects on Health No ill effects are reported, although as a synthetic azo-dye, it may affect hyperactive children and those who suffer from asthma or are aspirin sensitive.

E471 Mono- and Di-glycerides of Fatty Acids

Stabilises and emulsifies.
Effects on Health No health risk known.

E435 Polyoxyethylene (20) Sorbitan Monostearate

Emulsifies and stabilises.
Effects on Health This substance may increase the absorption of liquid paraffin and other fat soluble items.

621 Monosodium Glutamate

Enhances the flavour of foods containing protein by stimulating the taste buds or increasing the degree of saliva produced in the mouth.
Effects on Health Responsible for symptoms of palpitation, headache, dizziness, nausea, muscle tightness, a feeling of weakness in the forearms, pains in the neck, and other, migraine-like symptoms in some people. This substance is recommended to be excluded from the diets of hyperactive children. It is also taboo in or on foods intended for babies and young children.

631 Sodium Inosinate

Enhances flavour.
Effects on Health This is taboo in or on foods made specially for babies and young children. It should be avoided by people who suffer from gout and related problems requiring the avoidance of purines. It is also recommended to be excluded from the diets of hyperactive children by the Hyperactive Children's Support Group. It can cause problems for asthmatics or those who are aspirin sensitive.

637 Guanosine 5′ Enhances flavour.

Effects on Health This is taboo in or on foods made specially for babies and young children. It should be avoided by people who suffer from gout and related problems requiring the avoidance of purines. It is also recommended to be excluded from the diets of hyperactive children by the Hyperactive Children's Support Group. It can cause problems for asthmatics or those who are aspirin sensitive.

Flavouring

Effects on Health Debatable, as no information is available. Many substances in this category are artificially synthesised; safety cannot be assumed.

Horseradish Sauce

COLMAN'S HORSERADISH SAUCE
*Sugar***   *Salt***

'Stabiliser' (Will be specified after January 1986). Possibly **E412 Guar Gum** Used as a thickener and emulsion stabiliser.
or
E415 Xanthan Gum Stabiliser and emulsifier.
Effects on Health No known ill effects. If guar gum is consumed to excess, effects could include nausea, stomach cramps and flatulence.
or
E413 Tragacanth Used to emulsify, stabilise and thicken.
Effects on Health Usually no ill effects although when tragacanth has been used on the skin contact dermatitis has occasionally resulted. If consumed in quantity, can cause stomach pain and swelling.

'Preservative' Possibly **223 Sodium Metabisulphite**, to be specified after January 1986. A preservative and antioxidant.
Effects on Health A member of the sulphite family which is harmful to asthmatics; may cause gastric irritation because of the liberation of sulphurous acid. Can cause allergies and food aversion.
or

E260 Acetic Acid A preservative that is antibacterial and dilutes colouring matter.
Effects on Health No known health risk.

BURGESS HORSERADISH SAUCE
*Sugar***   *Salt***

E412 Guar Gum Used as a thickener and emulsion stabiliser.
Effects on Health No known health risk unless consumed to excess when nausea, stomach cramps and flatulence might result.

E415 Xanthan Gum Used to stabilise and emulsify.
Effects on Health No known health risk, unless consumed in quantity.

E171 Titanium Dioxide Provides white colour to surface of product.
Effects on Health No health risks known.

E102 Tartrazine Gives yellow colour to food.
Effects on Health Has been implicated with causing sleeplessness at night in hyperactive and food-sensitive children. Symptoms including skin rash, hay fever, problems with breathing, blurred vision

and purple skin patches are reported in susceptible people, particularly those who are aspirin sensitive or asthmatic.

E334 Tartaric Acid Used as an antioxidant or synergist i.e. to enhance the antioxidant effect of other substances; dilutes food colouring.
Effects on Health No known health risk if taken in usual quantities. Undiluted tartaric acid might cause gastro-enteritis.

E270 Lactic Acid Used to preserve and to increase the antioxidant effect of other substances. Also flavours.
Effects on Health Very young or premature babies may have trouble metabolising lactic acid. No health risks known for adults.

Flavouring
Effects on Health Debatable, as no information is available. Many substances in this category are artificially synthesised; safety cannot be assumed.

SAINSBURY'S HORSE-RADISH SAUCE
Sugar***   *Salt***

E260 Acetic Acid A preservative that is antibacterial and dilutes colouring matter.
Effects on Health No known health risk.

E465 Ethylmethylcellulose Used to stabilise or emulsify; a foaming agent.
Effects on Health No known health risks.

E412 Guar Gum Used as a thickener and emulsion stabiliser.
Effects on Health No known health risk unless consumed to excess when nausea, stomach cramps or flatulence might result.

E415 Xanthan Gum Stabiliser and emulsifier.
Effects on Health No known health risks unless gums are consumed in quantity.

E334 Tartaric Acid Used as an antioxidant or synergist i.e. to enhance the antioxidant effect of other substances; dilutes food colouring.
Effects on Health No known health risk if taken in usual quantities. Undiluted tartaric acid might cause gastro-enteritis.

E223 Sodium Metabisulphite A preservative and antioxidant.
Effects on Health A member of the sulphite family which is harmful to asthmatics; may cause gastric irritation because of the liberation of sulphurous acid. Can cause allergies and food aversion.

Flavouring
Effects on Health Debatable, as no information is available. Many substances in this category are artificially synthesised; safety cannot be assumed.

E320 Butylated Hydroxyanisole As an antioxidant this works alone or in conjunction with a synergist, i.e. citric acid or phosphoric acid, which enhances its effect. It prevents rancidity and also delays flavour deterioration due to oxidation.

Effects on Health It raises the lipid and cholesterol levels in the blood. Because it encourages the formation of metabolising enzymes in the liver there is the increased risk of breakdown of important substances in the body such as vitamin D. The Hyperactive Children's Support Group recommend that this is not included in the diet of food-sensitive children. It is not permitted in foods intended for babies and young children with the exception of its use to preserve added vitamin A.

E321 Butylated Hydroxytoluene Used as an antioxidant for food fats and oils.

Effects on Health Those who are sensitive to this antioxidant may develop rashes. It can increase the rate of breakdown of other substances in the body, i.e. vitamin D, because of the development of metabolising enzymes. Other reports link this additive with a possibility of reproductive failures, blood cell changes and effects on behaviour. The Hyperactive Children's Support Group include this on the list of substances not recommended for food-sensitive children; it is taboo in foods intended for babies and young children with the exception of its use to preserve added vitamin A. There have been conflicting research reports on its effects on rats.

also

WAITROSE HORSERADISH SAUCE

Ice Cream—Vanilla Flavour

LOSELEY

*Sugar*** *   Salt*

Stabiliser of Vegetable Origin

Emulsifier of Vegetable Origin (Will be specified from January 1986). Possibly **E401 Sodium Alginate** or **E410 Locust Bean Gum**

Effects on Health No known ill effects.

or

E407 Carrageenan Used to thicken, emulsify or as a gelling agent.

Effects on Health It has been reported as a possible cause of ulcerative colitis and when degraded may be carcinogenic.

TESCO

Sugar**   *Salt*

E471 Mono- and Di-glycerides of Fatty Acids
An emulsifier and stabiliser.
Effects on Health Not known as a health risk.

E410 Locust Bean Gum Used to stabilise and emulsify; also a gelling agent.
Effects on Health There are no known health risks. Pods of the bean have been consumed since Biblical times. Refined gums may cause stomach pain or swelling if consumed in quantity.

E407 Carrageenan Used to thicken, emulsify or as a gelling agent.
Effects on Health It has been reported as a possible cause of ulcerative colitis and when degraded may be carcinogenic.

E102 Tartrazine Gives yellow colouring to product.
Effects on Health Has been implicated with causing sleeplessness at night in hyperactive and food-sensitive children. Symptoms including skin rash, hay fever, problems with breathing, blurred vision and purple skin patches are reported in susceptible people, particularly those who are aspirin sensitive or asthmatic.

E110 Sunset Yellow FCF
Gives yellow colouring to product.
Effects on Health One of the azo-dye family which is recommended to be excluded from the diets of hyperactive children. Adults may have an allergic reaction with symptoms of skin rash, swollen blood vessels and gastric problems, especially if aspirin sensitive.

WALL'S BLUE RIBBON

Sugar***   *Salt*

E471 Mono- and Di-glycerides of Fatty Acids
An emulsifier and stabiliser.
Effects on Health Not known as a health risk.

E401 Sodium Alginate
Stabilises, thickens and emulsifies.
Effects on Health Not known as a health risk.

E407 Carrageenan Used to thicken, emulsify, or as a gelling agent.
Effects on Health It has been reported as a possible cause of ulcerative colitis and when degraded may be carcinogenic.

E410 Locust Bean Gum Used to stabilise and emulsify, also a gelling agent.
Effects on Health There are no known health risks. Pods of the bean have been consumed since Biblical times. Refined gums may cause stomach pain or swelling if consumed in quantity.

E412 Guar Gum Thickener and dietary bulker.
Effects on Health Harmless except in excess when stomach cramps,

nausea and flatulence might
result.

E102 Tartrazine Gives yellow
colouring to product.
Effects on Health Has been
implicated with causing
sleeplessness at night in
hyperactive and food-sensitive
children. Symptoms including
skin rash, hay fever, problems
with breathing, blurred vision
and purple skin patches are
reported in susceptible people,
particularly those who are
aspirin sensitive or asthmatic.

E110 Sunset Yellow FCF
Gives yellow colouring to
product.
Effects on Health One of the azo-
dye family which is
recommended to be excluded
from the diets of hyperactive
children. Adults may have
allergic reactions with symptoms
of skin rash, swollen blood
vessels and gastric problems,
especially if aspirin sensitive.

also

LYONS MAID
Sugar***   *Salt**

CO-OP
Sugar*   *Salt*

Plus (for Lyons Maid and Co-op):
Flavouring
Effects on Health Debatable, as
no information is available.
Many substances in this
category are artificially
synthesised; safety cannot be
assumed.

SAINSBURY'S
Sugar***   *Salt*

**E471 Mono- and Di-
glycerides of Fatty Acids**
Emulsifier and stabiliser.
Effects on Health Not known as a
health risk.

E401 Sodium Alginate
Stabilises, thickens and
emulsifies.
Effects on Health Not known as a
health risk.

**E339 Sodium Dihydrogen
Orthophosphate** Used to
enhance the effects of other
antioxidants, as a texture
improver and to balance
acidity/alkalinity at a
determined level.
Effects on Health Not known as a
health risk.

E460 Alpha-cellulose Prevents
particles sticking together, binds
or adds bulk and thickens.
Effects on Health A substance not
permitted to be used in foods
intended for babies and young
children. No other ill effects
known.

E104 Quinoline Yellow Gives
a greenish-yellow colour to food.
Effects on Health This is a synthetic
dye of the azo-dye family and
therefore is not recommended by
the Hyperactive Children's
Support Group for inclusion in
the diets of susceptible
children.

E110 Sunset Yellow FCF
Gives yellow colouring to
food.

Effects on Health One of the azo-dye family which is recommended to be excluded from the diets of hyperactive children. Adults may have an allergic reaction with symptoms of skin rash, swollen blood vessels and gastric problems, especially if aspirin sensitive.

Flavouring
Effects on Health Debatable, as no information is available. Many substances in this category are artificially synthesised; safety cannot be assumed.

Instant Mashed Potatoes

YEOMAN MASHED POTATOES
*Sugar   Salt*****

E471 Mono- and Di-glycerides of Fatty Acids
An emulsifier and stabiliser.
Effects on Health Not known as a health risk.

E450(a) Tetrasodium Diphosphate Maintains acidity/alkalinity at a determined level; an emulsifying salt and stabiliser, also gelling agent.
Effects on Health Not known as a health risk.

E223 Sodium Metabisulphite
Used as an antioxidant and to preserve.
Effects on Health A member of the sulphite family which is harmful to asthmatics; may cause gastric irritation because of the freeing of sulphurous acids. Can cause food allergies and aversions.

E321 Butylated Hydroxytoluene Used as an antioxidant for food fats and oils.
Effects on Health Those who are sensitive to this antioxidant may develop rashes. It can increase the rate of breakdown of other substances in the body, i.e. vitamin D, because of the development of metabolising enzymes. Other reports link this additive with a possibility of reproductive failures, blood cell changes and effects on behaviour. The Hyperactive Children's Support Group include this on the list of substances not recommended for food-sensitive children; it is taboo in foods intended for babies and young children with the exception of its use to preserve added vitamin A. There have been conflicting research reports on its effect on rats.

SAFEWAY INSTANT MASHED POTATO

Sugar   Salt**

E471 Mono- and Di-glycerides and Fatty Acids
An emulsifier and stabiliser.
Effects on Health Not known as a health risk.

E450(a) Tetrasodium Diphosphate Maintains acidity/alkalinity at a determined level; an emulsifying salt and stabiliser, also gelling agent.
Effects on Health Not known as a health risk

E223 Sodium Metabisulphite Used as an antioxidant and to preserve.
Effects on Health A member of the sulphite family which is harmful to asthmatics; may cause gastric irritation because of the freeing of sulphurous acids. Can cause food allergies and aversions.

E320 Butylated Hydroxyanisole As an antioxidant this works alone or in conjunction with a synergist, i.e. citric acid or phosphoric acid, which enhances its effect. It prevents rancidity and also delays flavour deterioration due to oxidation.
Effects on Health It raises the lipid and cholesterol levels in the blood. Because it encourages the formation of metabolising enzymes in the liver there is the increased risk of breakdown of important substances in the body such as vitamin D. The Hyperactive Children's Support Group recommend that this is not included in the diet of food-sensitive children. It is not permitted in foods intended for babies and young children with the exception of its use to preserve added vitamin A.

E321 Butylated Hydroxytoluene Used as an antioxidant for food fats and oils.
Effects on Health Those who are sensitive to this antioxidant may develop rashes. It can increase the rate of breakdown of other substances in the body, i.e. vitamin D, because of the development of metabolising enzymes. Other reports link this additive with a possibility of reproductive failures, blood cell changes and effects on behaviour. The Hyperactive Children's Support Group include this on the list of substances not recommended for food-sensitive children; it is taboo in foods intended for babies and young children with the exception of its use to preserve added vitamin A. There have been conflicting re-search reports on its effect on rats.

also

CO-OP

CADBURY'S SMASH

See Note p. v

Jam Tarts

HALES TRADITIONAL JAM TARTS
Sugar***   *Salt*

E440(a) Pectin Emulsifier and gelling agent.
Effects on Health No adverse effects although large amounts could cause temporary stomach distension or flatulence.

Flavouring
Effects on Health Debatable, as no information is available. Many substances in this category are artificially synthesised; safety cannot be assumed.

'Colour' undefined by 'E' numbers until January 1986, but could be **E102, E110, E122, E124**
Effects on Health All are synthetic azo-dyes which have been excluded in the dietary recommendations of the Hyperactive Children's Support Group. They are also implicated with causing allergic reactions in susceptible people such as those who are aspirin sensitive or asthmatic.

SAINSBURY'S JAM TARTS
Sugar***   *Salt**

E440(a) Pectin Emulsifier and gelling agent.
Effects on Health No adverse effects although large amounts could cause temporary stomach distension or flatulence.

E330 Citric Acid Stabilises the acidity of food substances, prevents discoloration of fruit, keeps the flavour 'true' and retains vitamin C.
Effects on Health Needs to be consumed in very large quantities to erode teeth or irritate locally.

E331 Sodium Citrates Acts as a synergist, i.e. enhances the effects of other antioxidants, an emulsifying salt and controls acid/alkaline levels.
Effects on Health Not known as a health risk.

E122 Carmoisine Gives red colouring to food.
Effects on Health This has been recommended by the Hyperactive Children's Support Group as unsuitable for children who are food sensitive. An azo-dye, it may produce adverse

reactions in people who have an aspirin allergy or are asthmatic. Such reactions can include skin rashes or swelling.

E102 Tartrazine Gives yellow colouring to food.
Effects on Health Has been implicated with causing sleeplessness at night in hyperactive and food-sensitive children. Symptoms including skin rashes, hay fever, problems with breathing, blurred vision and purple skin patches are reported in susceptible people, particularly those who are aspirin sensitive or asthmatic.

E110 Sunset Yellow FCF Gives yellow colouring to food.
Effects on Health One of the azo-dye family which is recommended to be excluded from the diets of hyperactive children. Adults may have an allergic reaction with symptoms of skin rash, swollen blood vessels and gastric problems, especially if aspirin sensitive.

E142 Acid Brilliant Green Gives green colouring to food.
Effects on Health No ill effects reported although as a synthetic azo-dye it may affect hyperactive children and those who suffer from asthma or are aspirin sensitive.

E202 Potassium Sorbate A preservative which is antifungal and antibacterial.
Effects on Health No known ill effects.

Plus (for Waitrose):

Flavouring
Effects on Health Debatable, as no information is available. Many substances in this category are artificially synthesised; safety cannot be assumed.

similar

WAITROSE JAM TARTS

LYONS JAM TARTS
Sugar***   *Salt***

E440(a) Pectin Emulsifier and gelling agent.
Effects on Health No adverse effects although large amounts could cause temporary stomach distension or flatulence.

Flavouring
Effects on Health Debatable, as no information is available. Many substances in this category are artificially synthesised; safety cannot be assumed.

E102 Tartrazine Gives yellow colouring to food.
Effects on Health Has been implicated with causing sleeplessness at night in hyperactive and food-sensitive children. Symptoms including skin rashes, hay fever, problems with breathing, blurred vision and purple skin patches are reported in susceptible people, particularly those who are aspirin sensitive or asthmatic.

E110 Sunset Yellow FCF
Gives yellow colouring to
food.
Effects on Health One of the azo-
dye family which is
recommended to be excluded
from the diets of hyperactive
children. Adults may have an
allergic reaction with symptoms
of skin rash, swollen blood
vessels and gastric problems,
especially if aspirin sensitive.

E122 Carmoisine Gives red
colouring to food.
Effects on Health This has been
recommended by the
Hyperactive Children's Support
Group as unsuitable for children
who are food sensitive. An azo-
dye, it may produce adverse
reactions in people who have
aspirin allergy or are asthmatic.
Such reactions can include skin
rashes or swelling.

E124 Ponceau 4R One of the
azo-dye family which is
recommended to be excluded
from the diets of hyperactive
children. Adults who are aspirin
sensitive or asthmatic may be
affected.

E142 Acid Brilliant Green
Gives green colouring to food.

Effects on Health No ill effects
reported although, as a
synthetic azo-dye, it may affect
hyperactive children and those
who suffer from asthma or are
aspirin sensitive.

E150 Caramel Gives brown
colouring to food and is used
as a flavouring.
Effects on Health A question
mark as to its safety hangs over
this additive. There has been a
reduction in the number of
kinds available to the food
industry. Work is in hand to
discover the safest form. One type
which is produced with ammonia
has been shown to cause vitamin
B6 deficiency in rats.

**E160(a) Alpha-carotene,
Beta-carotene, Gamma-
carotene** Gives an orange-
yellow colour to food and
converts to vitamin A in the
body.
Effects on Health No known
health risks.

E202 Potassium Sorbate A
preservative which is antifungal
and antibacterial.
Effects on Health No known ill
effects.

Lemon Curd

WAITROSE LEMON CHEESE
*Sugar*** *Salt*

E330 Citric Acid Stabilises the acidity of food substances, prevents discoloration of fruit, keeps the flavour 'true' and retains vitamin C.
Effects on Health Needs to be consumed in very large quantities to erode teeth or irritate locally.

CO-OP LEMON CURD
*Sugar*** *Salt**

E330 Citric Acid Stabilises the acidity of food substances, prevents discoloration of fruit, keeps the flavour 'true' and retains vitamin C.
Effects on Health Needs to be consumed in very large quantities to erode teeth or irritate locally.

E331 Sodium Citrates Acts as a synergist, i.e. enhances the effects of other antioxidants, an emulsifying salt and controls acid/alkaline levels.
Effects on Health Not known as a health risk.

E440(a) Pectin Emulsifier and gelling agent.
Effects on Health No adverse effects although large amounts could cause temporary stomach distension or flatulence.

E102 Tartrazine Gives yellow colouring to product.
Effects on Health Has been implicated with causing sleeplessness at night in hyperactive and food-sensitive children. Symptoms including skin rashes, hay fever, problems with breathing, blurred vision and purple skin patches are reported in susceptible people, particularly those who are aspirin sensitive or asthmatic.

E171 Titanium Dioxide Gives a white colouring to the surface of a product.
Effects on Health No known health risk.

Plus (for Wiltshire):
Modified Starch Used as thickener. An umbrella term for 18 substances not defined by 'E' numbers.
Effects on Health No suggestion that they are harmful.

also
WILTSHIRE LEMON CURD
*Sugar*** *Salt*

SAFEWAY LEMON CURD

Sugar**   *Salt**

E440(a) Pectin Emulsifier and gelling agent.
Effects on Health No adverse effects although large amounts could cause temporary stomach distension or flatulence.

E330 Citric Acid Stabilises the acidity of food substances, prevents discoloration of fruit, keeps the flavour 'true' and retains vitamin C.
Effects on Health Needs to be consumed in very large quantities to erode teeth or irritate locally.

Emulsifier Yet to be specified. Possibly **E471 Mono- and Di-glycerides of Fatty Acids** Emulsifier and stabiliser.
Effects on Health Not known as a health risk.

E102 Tartrazine Gives yellow colouring to product.
Effects on Health Has been implicated with causing sleeplessness at night in hyperactive and food-sensitive children. Symptoms including skin rashes, hay fever, problems with breathing, blurred vision and purple skin patches are reported in susceptible people, particularly those who are aspirin sensitive or asthmatic.

E220 Sulphur Dioxide Used as a preservative, an antioxidant,

and to stabilise vitamin C; also improving and bleaching agent.
Effects on Health Possibility that it can irritate the alimentary food canal. Destroys much of the vitamin E content in flour. The Hyperactive Children's Support Group do not recommend this substance in susceptible children's diets.

SAINSBURY'S LEMON CURD

Sugar**   *Salt**

Modified Starch Used as thickener. An umbrella term for 18 substances not defined by 'E' numbers.
Effects on Health No suggestion that they are harmful.

E330 Citric Acid Stabilises the acidity of food substances, prevents discoloration of fruit, keeps the flavour 'true' and retains vitamin C.
Effects on Health Needs to be consumed in very large quantities to erode teeth or irritate locally.

E260 Acetic Acid
Antibacterial, used to stabilise the acidity of food and dilute colouring matter.
Effects on Health No known ill effects.

E102 Tartrazine Gives yellow colouring to product.

Effects on Health Has been implicated with causing sleeplessness at night in hyperactive and food-sensitive children. Symptoms including skin rashes, hay fever, problems with breathing, blurred vision and purple skin patches are reported in susceptible people, particularly those who are aspirin sensitive or asthmatic.

E110 Sunset Yellow FCF
Gives yellow colouring to product.
Effects on Health One of the azo-dye family which is

recommended to be excluded from the diets of hyperactive children. Adults may have an allergic reaction with symptoms of skin rash, swollen blood vessels and gastric problems, especially if aspirin sensitive.

E124 Ponceau 4R Gives red colouring to product.
Effects on Health One of the azo-dye family which is recommended to be excluded from the diets of hyperactive children. Adults who are aspirin sensitive or asthmatic may be affected.

Malted Drinks

HORLICKS INSTANT
*Sugar*** *Salt***

501 Potassium Carbonate
Used to balance alkaline/acid levels.
Effects on Health Not known as a health risk.

TESCO MALTED DRINK
*Sugar*** *Salt**

500 Sodium Bicarbonate
Used to balance alkaline/acid levels and to aerate.
Effects on Health Not known as a health risk.

501 Potassium Carbonate
Used to balance alkaline/acid levels.
Effects on Health Not known as a health risk.

also

WAITROSE MALTED DRINK

SAFEWAY

SAINSBURY'S MALTED DRINK
*Sugar** *   *Salt**

500 Sodium Bicarbonate Used to balance alkaline/acid levels and to aerate.
Effects on Health Not known as a health risk.

501 Potassium Carbonate Used to balance alkaline/acid levels.
Effects on Health Not known as a health risk.

E322 Lecithin Acts as an emulsifier and stabiliser; it is an antioxidant and gives additional thickness to fats.
Effects on Health There are no known health risks; in fact, lecithin is used therapeutically to mobilise fats in the body and has also been experimented with in the treatment of senile dementia.

OVALTINE INSTANT
*Sugar****   *Salt*

E471 Mono- and Di-glycerides of Fatty Acids An emulsifier and stabiliser.
Effects on Health Not known as a health risk.

'Stabiliser' Yet to be specified.
Effects on Health This group is not associated with appreciable health risk.

Flavouring
Effects on Health Debatable, as no information is available. Many substances in this category are artificially synthesised; safety cannot be assumed.

Margarine

TOMOR KOSHER
Sugar   *Salt** *

'Colour' possibly **E160(a) Alpha-carotene, Beta-carotene, Gamma-carotene** Gives orange-yellow colour to product and converts to vitamin A in the body.
Effects on Health No known health risk.

or
E160(b) Annatto Bixin Norbixin Gives a yellow to peach colour to product.
Effects on Health Safe except in the case of hives reported in some people.

Flavouring
Effects on Health Debatable, as no information is available. Many substances in this category are artificially synthesised; safety cannot be assumed.

KRAFT SUPERFINE
*Sugar   Salt***

E471 Mono- and Di-glycerides of Fatty Acids
Used to emulsify and stabilise.
Effects on Health No known
health risk.

E322 Lecithin Acts as an
emulsifier and stabiliser; it is
also an antioxidant and gives
additional thickness to fats.
Effects on Health There are no
known health risks; in fact lecithin
is used therapeutically to mobilise
fats in the body and has also been
experimented with in the
treatment of senile dementia.

Flavouring
Effects on Health Debatable, as
no information is available.
Many substances in this
category are artificially
synthesised; safety cannot be
assumed.

E160(a) Alpha-carotene, Beta-carotene, Gamma-carotene
Gives yellow-orange colour to
product; converts to vitamin A
in the body.
Effects on Health There are no
known health risks.

similarly

FLORA

STORK

BLUE BAND

SAINSBURY'S

CO-OP GOOD LIFE

OUTLINE
Sugar   Salt

**E160(b) Annatto Bixin
Norbixin** Gives a yellow to
peach colour to product.
Effects on Health Safe except for
reports of hives in some people.

E471 Mono- and Di-glycerides of Fatty Acids
Used to emulsify or stabilise.
Effects on Health No known
health risk.

E202 Potassium Sorbate A
preservative that is antifungal
and antibacterial.
Effects on Health Not known as a
health risk.

E270 Lactic Acid Used to
preserve and also increases the
antioxidant effect of other
substances; flavours product.
Effects on Health Very young or
premature babies may have
trouble metabolising lactic acid.
No health risks known for
adults.

Flavouring
Effects on Health Debatable, as
no information is available.
Many substances in this
category are artificially
synthesised; safety cannot be
assumed.

ST IVEL GOLD
Sugar   Salt**

E325 Sodium Lactate
Enhances the antioxidant effect
of other substances; prevents
food from drying.
Effects on Health Possibility of
adverse effect for very young
children; for adults, no known
health risk.

E331 Sodium Citrates Acts as
synergist, i.e. enhances the
effects of other antioxidants, an
emulsifying salt and controls the
acid/alkaline level.
Effects on Health No known
health risk.

**E339 Sodium Dihydrogen
Orthophosphate** Used to
enhance effects of other
antioxidants, as a texture
improver and to balance
acid/alkalinity at a determined
level.

Effects on health No known
health risks.

**E471 Mono- and Di-
glycerides of Fatty Acids**
Used to emulsify or stabilise.
Effects on Health No known
health risks.

E202 Potassium Sorbate A
preservative that is antifungal
and antibacterial.
Effects on Health No known
health risk.

Flavouring
Effects on Health Debatable, as
no information is available.
Many substances in this
category are artificially
synthesised; safety cannot be
assumed.

**E160(a) Alpha-carotene, Beta-
carotene, Gamma-carotene**
Gives orange-yellow colour to
product and converts to vitamin
A in the body.
Effects on Health No known
health risk.

Marmalade

CO-OP ORANGE
JELLY SHREDLESS
Sugar***   Salt

E440(a) Pectin Emulsifier and
gelling agent.
Effects on Health No adverse
effects although large amounts
could cause temporary stomach
distension or flatulence.

E330 Citric Acid Stabilises the
acidity of food substances,
prevents discoloration of fruit,
keeps the flavour 'true' and
retains vitamin C.
Effects on Health Needs to be
consumed in very large
quantities to erode teeth and
irritate locally.

Plus (for Sainsbury's and
Robertson's):

E331 Sodium Citrates Acts as a synergist, i.e. enhances the effects of other antioxidants, an emulsifying salt and controls the acid/alkaline level.
Effects on Health No known health risk.

also

FINE FARE ORANGE JELLY

similar

SAINSBURY'S ORANGE SHRED

ROBERTSON'S SILVER SHRED

Sugar**   *Salt*

CHIVERS BREAKFAST MARMALADE

Sugar***   *Salt*

E440(a) Pectin Emulsifier and gelling agent.
Effects on Health No adverse effects although large amounts could cause temporary stomach flatulence or distension.

E331 Sodium Citrates Acts as a synergist, i.e. enhances the effects of other antioxidants, an emulsifying salt and controls acid/alkaline level.
Effects on Health No known health risk.

E150 Caramel Gives brown colouring to product and is used as a flavouring.
Effects on Health A question

mark as to its safety hangs over this additive. There has been a reduction in the number of kinds available to the food industry. Work is in hand to discover the safest form. One kind is produced with ammonia which has been shown to cause vitamin B6 deficiency in rats.

SAFEWAY MEDIUM CUT ORANGE MARMALADE

Sugar***   *Salt*

E440(a) Pectin Emulsifier and gelling agent.
Effects on Health No adverse effects although large amounts could cause temporary stomach distension or flatulence.

E330 Citric Acid Stabilises the acidity of food substances, prevents discoloration of fruit, keeps the flavour 'true' and retains vitamin C.
Effects on Health Needs to be consumed in very large quantities to erode teeth and irritate locally.

E220 Sulphur Dioxide Used to preserve and as an antioxidant; stabilises vitamin C.
Effects on Health Possibility of irritation of the alimentary food canal. It is also one of the substances on the list of additives which are recommended to be avoided by hyperactive children.

Marzipan

SHARWOOD'S

Sugar***   *Salt*

No artificial colouring

WHITWORTHS

Sugar***   *Salt*

E102 Tartrazine Gives yellow colouring to product.
Effects on Health Has been implicated with causing sleeplessness at night in hyperactive and food-sensitive children. Symptoms including skin rashes, hay fever, problems with breathing, blurred vision and purple skin patches are reported in susceptible people, particularly those who are aspirin sensitive or asthmatic.

E110 Sunset Yellow FCF Gives yellow colouring to product.
Effects on Health One of the azo-dye family which is recommended to be excluded from the diets of hyperactive children. Adults may have an allergic reaction with symptoms of skin rash, swollen blood vessels and gastric problems, especially if aspirin sensitive.

E122 Carmoisine Gives red colouring to product.
Effects on Health This has been recommended by the Hyperactive Children's Support Group as unsuitable for children who are food sensitive. An azo-dye, it may produce adverse reactions in people who have an aspirin allergy or are asthmatic. Such reactions can include skin rashes or swelling.

also

SAINSBURY

SAFEWAY

Meat Pastes and Spreads

GATEWAY BEEF AND HAM

Sugar   *Salt***

E300 Ascorbic Acid Acts as an antioxidant in emulsion of fats and oils; inhibits browning action in unprocessed fruits, fruit pulps and juices; preserves meat colour.
Effects on Health Taken in very large doses it may induce diarrhoea or erode teeth. Susceptible people could develop kidney stones if substance was taken in a daily dose in excess of 10g.

SAINSBURY'S BEEF SPREAD

Sugar   *Salt***

E450(a) Tetrasodium Diphosphate Maintains acidity/alkalinity at a determined level; an emulsifying salt and stabiliser, also gelling agent.
Effects on Health No health risks known.

E450(b) Pentasodium Triphosphate Used to provide texture and is an emulsifying salt.
Effects on Health French research suggests that polyphosphates can block a number of enzymes, causing digestive disturbances.

E250 Sodium Nitrite Preserves food and inhibits the growth of bacterium responsible for botulism.
Effects on Health Nitrites may interact with amines from foods in the stomach to form nitrosamines which are known to cause cancer in animals. They are taboo in foods for babies and young children. Such an additive can cause allergic reactions and is on the list of foods not recommended by the Hyperactive Children's Support Group.

also

SUTHERLANDS BEEF SPREAD

SHIPPAMS BEEF PASTE

Sugar   Salt**

'Colour' as yet unspecified, possibly **E150 Caramel** Gives brown colouring to product and is used as a flavouring.
Effects on Health A question mark as to its safety hangs over this additive. There has been a reduction in the number of kinds available to the food industry. Work is in hand to discover the safest form. One kind which is produced with ammonia has been shown to cause vitamin B6 deficiency in rats.

also

SAFEWAY BEEF PASTE

PRINCES BEEF SPREAD

SAINSBURY'S POTTED BEEF

Sugar   Salt**

621 Monosodium Glutamate Enhances the flavour of foods containing protein by stimulating the taste buds or increasing degree of saliva produced in the mouth.
Effects on Health Responsible for symptoms of palpitation, headache, dizziness, nausea, muscle tightness, a feeling of weakness in the forearms, pains in the neck, and other, migraine-like symptoms in some people. This substance is recommended to be excluded from the diets of hyperactive children; it is also taboo in or on foods intended for babies and young children.

Milk Shake Mixes

NESQUIK MILK SHAKE MIX

Sugar***   Salt

E330 Citric Acid Stabilises the acidity of fruit substances, prevents discoloration of fruit, keeps the flavour 'true' and retains vitamin C.

Effects on Health Needs to be taken in very large quantities to erode teeth or cause irritation.

Flavouring
Effects on Health Debatable, as no information is available. Many substances in this category are artificially synthesised; safety cannot be assumed.

'**Colour**' as yet unspecified, possibly **E122** or **E128 Carmoisine** or **Red 2G**.
Effects on Health These are synthetic azo-dyes and therefore are suspect for people who have aspirin sensitivity or are asthmatic. These additives are recommended by the Hyperactive Children's Support Group to be excluded from the diets of such children.

'**Antioxidant**' as yet unspecified, possibly **E300 Lecithin** Acts as an emulsifier and stabiliser; it is also an antioxidant and gives additional thickness to fats.
Effects on Health There are no known health risks; in fact, lecithin is used therapeutically to mobilise fats in the body and has also been experimented with in the treatment of senile dementia.

EDEN VALE SUPER SHAKE
Sugar   Salt

E415 Corn Sugar Gum Used to stabilise or thicken.
Effects on Health There are no known health risks.

E412 Guar Gum Used to thicken, a bulking agent.
Effects on Health Harmless except when consumed to excess when nausea, flatulence and stomach cramps might occur.

Flavouring
Effects on Health Debatable, as

no information is available. Many substances in this category are artificially synthesised; safety cannot be assumed.

E124 Ponceau 4R Gives red colouring to product.
Effects on Health One of the azo-dye family which is recommended to be excluded from the diets of hyperactive children. Adults who are aspirin sensitive or asthmatic may be affected.

SAINSBURY'S AMERICAN STYLE THICK MILK SHAKE MIX
Sugar***   Salt

E407 Carrageenan Used to thicken, emulsify or as a gelling agent.
Effects on Health It has been reported as a possible cause of ulcerative colitis and when degraded may be carcinogenic.

E415 Corn Sugar Gum Used to stabilise or thicken.
Effects on Health There are no known health risks.

E401 Sodium Alginate Stabilises, thickens and emulsifies.
Effects on Health No known health risks.

E477 Propane-1, 2-Diol Esters of Fatty Acids Used to emulsify or stabilise.

Effects on Health No known health risks.

Flavouring
Effects on Health Debatable, as no information is available. Many substances in this category are artificially synthesised; safety cannot be assumed.

E330 Citric Acid Stabilises the acidity of fruit substances, prevents discoloration of fruit, keeps the flavour 'true' and retains vitamin C.
Effects on Health Needs to be taken in very large quantities to erode teeth or cause irritation.

E128 Red 2G Gives red colour to product.
Effects on Health There is need for further research into the effects of this additive. It is one of the list that are recommended by the Hyperactive Children's Support Group to be excluded from the diets of food-sensitive children.

CRUSHA MILK SHAKE SYRUP
Sugar.***   *Salt*

E223 Sodium Metabisulphite
Used as an antioxidant and to preserve.
Effects on Health A member of the sulphite family which is harmful to asthmatics; may cause gastric irritation because of the freeing of sulphurous acid. Can cause food allergies and aversion.

Flavouring
Effects on Health Debatable, as no information is available. Many substances in this category are artificially synthesised; safety cannot be assumed.

E122 Carmoisine Gives red colouring to product.
Effects on Health This has been recommended by the Hyperactive Children's Support Group as unsuitable for children who are food sensitive. An azo-dye, it may produce adverse reactions in people who have aspirin sensitivity or are asthmatic. Such reactions can include skin rashes or swelling.

E110 Sunset Yellow FCF
Gives yellow colouring to product.
Effects on Health One of the azo-dye family which is recommended to be excluded from the diets of hyperactive children. Adults may have an allergic reaction with symptoms of skin rash, swollen blood vessels and gastric problems, especially if aspirin sensitive.

E102 Tartrazine Gives yellow colouring to product.
Effects on Health Has been implicated with causing sleeplessness at night in hyperactive and food-sensitive children. Symptoms including skin rashes, hay fever, problems with breathing, blurred vision and purple skin patches are reported in susceptible people, particularly those who are aspirin sensitive or asthmatic.

Minced Beef with Onions

SAINSBURY'S MINCED BEEF WITH ONIONS

Sugar*   *Salt***

Modified Starch Used as thickener. An umbrella term for 18 substances not defined by 'E' numbers.
Effects on Health No suggestion that they are harmful.

E150 Caramel Gives brown colouring to product and is used as a flavouring.
Effects on Health A question mark as to its safety hangs over this additive. There has been a reduction in the number of kinds available to the food industry. Work is in hand to discover the safest form. One type which is produced with ammonia has been shown to cause vitamin B6 deficiency in rats.

also

SUTHERLANDS MINCED STEAK WITH ONIONS AND GRAVY

Sugar   *Salt***

CO-OP

Sugar   *Salt**

621 Monosodium Glutamate
Enhances the flavour of foods containing protein by stimulating the taste buds or increasing the degree of saliva produced in the mouth.
Effects on Health Responsible for symptoms of palpitation, headache, dizziness, nausea, muscle tightness, a feeling of weakness in the forearms, pains in the neck, and other, migraine-like symptoms in some people. This substance is recommended to be excluded from the diets of hyperactive children; it is also taboo in or on foods intended for babies and young children.

E150 Caramel Gives brown colouring to product and is used as a flavouring.
Effects on Health A question mark as to its safety hangs over this additive. There has been a reduction in the number of kinds available to the food industry. Work is in hand to discover the safest form. One type which is produced with ammonia has been shown to cause vitamin B6 deficiency in rats.

E460 Alpha-cellulose Used to prevent food particles sticking together, to add bulk or bind, or as a thickening agent.
Effects on Health This additive is taboo in foods intended for babies and young children. No other health risks known.

similar

SMC MINCED BEEF WITH ONION AND GRAVY
(Minus E460)

Sugar **   *Salt* **

TYNE BRAND MINCED BEEF WITH ONIONS

Sugar   *Salt* **

Modified Starch Used as thickener. An umbrella term for 18 substances not defined by 'E' numbers.
Effects on Health No suggestion that they are harmful.

'Colour' possibly **E150 Caramel** Gives brown colouring to product and is used as a flavouring.
Effects on Health A question mark as to its safety hangs over this additive. There has been a reduction in the number of kinds available to the food

industry. Work is in hand to discover the safest form. One kind which is produced with ammonia has been shown to cause vitamin B6 deficiency in rats.

621 Monosodium Glutamate
Enhances the flavour of foods containing protein by stimulating the taste buds or increasing the degree of saliva produced in the mouth.
Effects on Health Responsible for symptoms of palpitation, headache, dizziness, nausea, muscle tightness, a feeling of weakness in the forearms, pains in the neck, and other, migraine-like symptoms in some people. This substance is recommended to be excluded from the diets of hyperactive children; it is also taboo in or on foods intended for babies and young children.

E450(c) Sodium Polyphosphates Emulsifying salts, used to stabilise.
Effects on Health French research suggests that polyphosphates might block a number of enzymes thus causing digestive disturbances.

Flavouring
Effects on Health Debatable, as no information is available. Many substances in this category are artificially synthesised; safety cannot be assumed.

Mincemeat

SAINSBURY'S MINCE-MEAT

Sugar***   *Salt**

E260 Acetic Acid Antibacterial, used to stabilise acidity of food and dilute colouring matter.
Effects on Health No known health risks.

CO-OP MINCEMEAT

Sugar**   *Salt*

E260 Acetic Acid Antibacterial, used to stabilise acidity of food and dilute colouring matter.
Effects on Health No known health risks.

E150 Caramel Gives brown colouring to product and is used as a flavouring.
Effects on Health A question mark as to its safety hangs over this additive. There has been a reduction in the number of kinds available to the food industry. Work is in hand to discover the safest form. One kind which is produced with ammonia has been shown to cause vitamin B6 deficiency in rats.

also

SAFEWAY MINCE-MEAT

Sugar**   *Salt***

WILTSHIRE MINCE-MEAT

ROBERTSON'S MINCE-MEAT

Sugar**   *Salt**

E260 Acetic Acid Antibacterial, used to stabilise acidity of food and dilute colouring matter.
Effects on Health No known health risks.

296 Malic Acid Used to flavour; an acid derived from apples.
Effects on Health No known health risks.

E150 Caramel Gives brown colouring to product and is used as a flavouring.
Effects on Health A question mark as to its safety hangs over this additive. There has been a reduction in the number of kinds available to the food industry. Work is in hand to discover the safest form. One kind which is produced with ammonia has been shown to cause vitamin B6 deficiency in rats.

Mint Sauce

COLMAN'S MINT SAUCE
Sugar   *Salt***

E260 Acetic Acid Antibacterial, used to stabilise the acidity of food and dilute colouring matter.
Effects on Health No known health effects.

'Colours' not yet specified, but possibly **E102 Tartrazine, E133 Brilliant Blue FCF.**
or
E142 Acid Brilliant Green
Gives green colouring to product.
Effects on Health All three are synthetic azo-dyes which have been recommended by the Hyperactive Children's Support Group to be excluded from the diets of hyperactive children. They may also cause adverse reactions in adults who are aspirin sensitive or suffer from asthma.

HP MINT SAUCE
*Sugar***   *Salt***

E405 Propane-1, 2-Diol Alginate Used to stabilise or emulsify and thicken; to disperse a substance in solution or suspension.
Effects on Health There are no known health risks.

E102 Tartrazine Gives yellow colouring to product.
Effects on Health One of the azo-dye family which is recommended to be excluded from the diets of hyperactive children. Adults may have an allergic reaction with symptoms of skin rash, swollen blood vessels and gastric problems, especially if aspirin sensitive.

E133 Brilliant Blue FCF
Provides a dark blue colouring which can convert to green tones when combined with tartrazine.
Effects on Health An azo-dye, it is a substance that has been recommended to be excluded from the diets of hyperactive children.

also

SAINSBURY'S MINT SAUCE

OK MINT SAUCE

Sugar**   *Salt***

E260 Acetic Acid Antibacterial
and used to stabilise the acidity
of food and dilute colouring
matter.
Effects on Health No known ill
effects.

'Stabiliser' possibly **E405
Propane-1, 2-Diol Alginate**
Used to stabilise, emulsify and
thicken, to disperse a substance
in solution or suspension.
Effects on Health There are no
known health risks.

'Colours' possibly **E102
Tartrazine, E133 Brilliant
Blue FCF.**
or
E142 Acid Brilliant Green
Gives green colouring to
product.
Effects on Health All three are
synthetic azo-dyes which have
been recommended by the
Hyperactive Children's Support
Group to be excluded from the
diets of hyperactive children.
They may also cause adverse
reactions in adults who are
aspirin sensitive or suffer from
asthma.

CO-OP MINT SAUCE

Sugar**   *Salt***

E260 Acetic Acid Antibacterial
and used to stabilise the acidity of
food and dilute colouring
matter.
Effects on Health No known ill
effects.

E412 Guar Gum Used as a
thickener or dietary bulker.
Effects on Health Harmless except
in excess when stomach cramps,
nausea and flatulence might
result.

E415 Corn Sugar Gum Used
to stabilise or thicken.
Effects on Health There are no
health risks known.

Flavouring
Effects on Health Debatable, as
no information is available.
Many substances in this
category are artificially
synthesised; safety cannot be
assumed.

E102 Tartrazine Gives yellow
colouring to product.
Effects on Health Has been
implicated with causing
sleeplessness at night in
hyperactive and food-sensitive
children. Symptoms including
skin rashes, hay fever, problems
with breathing, blurred vision
and purple skin patches are
reported in susceptible people,
particularly those who are
aspirin sensitive or asthmatic.

E142 Acid Brilliant Green A
member of the azo-dye family
which gives green colouring to
product.
Effects on Health No ill effects
reported although as a synthetic
dye it may affect hyperactive
children and those who suffer
from asthma or are aspirin
sensitive.

also

**SAFEWAY
CONCENTRATED
MINT SAUCE**

Muesli

KELLOGG'S
'SUMMER ORCHARD'

*No additives and no added sugar or
salt.*

KELLOGG'S
'COUNTRY STORE'
*Sugar*** *** *Salt*** **

No additives.

CO-OP
*Sugar*** ** *Salt*** **

No additives.

TESCO
WHOLEWHEAT
MUESLI
*Sugar*** ** *Salt*** *

E220 Sulphur Dioxide Used as
a preservative, antioxidant, and
to stabilise vitamin C; an
improving and bleaching agent.
Effects on Health Possibility that
it might irritate the alimentary
food canal. Destroys much of
the vitamin E content in flour.
The Hyperactive Children's
Support Group do not
recommend this substance in
susceptible children's diets.

Orange Squash

ST CLEMENT'S ORIGINAL ORANGE SQUASH

*Sugar***   *Salt*

296 Malic Acid Flavouring.
Effects on Health No harmful effects are known.

E223 Sodium Metabisulphite
A preservative and antioxidant.
Effects on Health A member of the sulphite family which is harmful to asthmatics; may cause gastric irritation because of the liberation of sulphurous acid; can cause allergies and food aversion.

E223 Sodium Metabisulphite
A preservative and antioxidant.
Effects on Health A member of the sulphite family which is harmful to asthmatics; may cause gastric irritation because of the liberation of sulphurous acid; can cause allergies and food aversion.

E211 Sodium Benzoate A preservative which is antibacterial and antifungal.
Effects on Health Can give problems of allergy to those who suffer from asthma or frequent skin rashes. Recommended to be excluded from the diets of hyperactive children.

SAINSBURY'S HIGH JUICE ORANGE SQUASH

*Sugar***   *Salt*

E330 Citric Acid Stabilises the acidity of food substances, prevents discoloration of fruit, keeps the flavour 'true' and retains vitamin C.
Effects on Health Needs to be consumed in very large quantities to erode teeth or irritate locally.

ROBINSONS ORANGE BARLEY WATER

*Sugar****   *Salt*

E330 Citric Acid Stabilises the acidity of food substances, prevents discoloration of fruit, keeps the flavours 'true' and retains vitamin C.
Effects on Health Needs to be consumed in very large quantities to erode teeth or irritate locally.

Flavouring
Effects on Health Debatable, as
no information is available.
Many substances in this
category are artificially
synthesised; safety cannot be
assumed.

'Preservatives' as yet
unspecified in this product but
might include **E223 Sodium
Metabisulphite** A preservative
and antioxidant.
Effects on Health A member of
the sulphite family which is
harmful to asthmatics; may
cause gastric irritation, because
of the liberation of sulphurous
acid; can cause allergies and
food aversions.

E211 Sodium Benzoate A
preservative which is
antibacterial and antifungal.
Effects on Health Can give
problems of allergy to those who
suffer from asthma or frequent
skin rashes. Recommended to be
excluded from the diets of
hyperactive children.

'Colours', as yet unspecified in
this product.
Effects on Health The
Hyperactive Children's Support
Group recommends all synthetic
colours should be excluded from
the diets of food-sensitive
children.

SAFEWAY ORANGE DRINK

Sugar***   *Salt*

E330 Citric Acid Stabilises the
acidity of food substances,
prevents discoloration of fruit,
keeps the flavour 'true' and
retains vitamin C.
Effects on Health Needs to be
consumed in very large
quantities to erode teeth or
irritate locally.

**E466
Carboxymethylcellulose,
Sodium Salt** Used as a
thickening agent and stabiliser.
Effects on Health Considered
'safe'.

E211 Sodium Benzoate A
preservative and antibacterial,
antifungal agent.
Effects on Health Can give
problems of allergy to those who
suffer from asthma or frequent
skin rashes. Recommended to be
excluded from the diets of
hyperactive children.

E223 Sodium Metabisulphite
A preservative and antioxidant.
Effects on Health A member of
the sulphite family which is
harmful to asthmatics; may
cause gastric irritation because
of the liberation of sulphurous
acid; can cause allergies and
food aversions.

E110 Sunset Yellow FCF
Colours food yellow.
Effects on Health One of the azo-

dye family which is recommended to be excluded from the diets of hyperactive children. Adults may have an allergic reaction with symptoms of skin rash, swollen blood vessels and gastric problems, especially if they are aspirin sensitive.

E102 Tartrazine Gives yellow colouring to product.

Effects on Health Has been implicated with causing sleeplessness at night in hyperactive and food-sensitive children. Symptoms including skin rashes, hay fever, problems with breathing, blurred vision, and purple skin patches are reported in susceptible people, particularly those who are aspirin sensitive or asthmatic.

Packet Tomato Soup

CROSSE & BLACKWELL'S SOUP IN BOXES
Sugar**   *Salt***

621 Monosodium Glutamate Enhances the flavour of foods containing protein by stimulating the taste buds or increasing the degree of saliva produced in the mouth.
Effects on Health Responsible for symptoms of palpitation, headache, dizziness, muscle tightness, nausea, feeling of weakness in the forearms, pains in the neck, and other, migraine-like symptoms in some people. This substance is recommended to be excluded from the diets of hyperactive children; it is also taboo in or on food intended for babies and young children.

'**Stabilisers**' as yet unspecified, possibly **E415 Xanthan Gum** or **E471 Mono- and Di-glycerides of Fatty Acids** or **E472 Lactic Acid Esters of Mono- and Di-glycerides of Fatty Acids**
Effects on Health No health risks known.

'**Colour**' as yet unspecified.
Effects on Health Many colourings are members of the azo-dye family, recommended by the Hyperactive Children's Support Group to be excluded from the diets of food-sensitive children; adults who are aspirin sensitive or asthmatic may also be affected.

E330 Citric Acid Stabilises the acidity of food substances, prevents discoloration of fruit, keeps the flavour 'true' and retains vitamin C.
Effects on Health Needs to be

consumed in very large
quantities to erode teeth or
irritate locally.

KNORR PACKET TOMATO
*Sugar***   *Salt**

Modified Starch Used as
thickener. An umbrella term for
18 substances not defined by 'E'
numbers.
Effects on Health No suggestion
that they are harmful.

**E320 Butylated
Hydroxyanisole** As an
antioxidant this works alone or
in conjunction with a synergist,
i.e. citric acid or phosphoric
acid, which enhances its effect.
It prevents rancidity and also
delays flavour deterioration due
to oxidation.
Effects on Health It raises the
lipid and cholesterol levels in
the blood. Because it encourages
the formation of metabolising
enzymes in the liver there is the
increased risk of the breakdown
of important substances in the
body such as vitamin D. The
Hyperactive Children's Support
Group recommend that this is
not included in the diet of food-
sensitive children. It is not
permitted in foods intended for
babies or young children, with
the exception of its use to
preserve added vitamin A.

621 Monosodium Glutamate
Enhances the flavour of foods
containing protein by
stimulating the taste buds or
increasing the degree of saliva
produced in the mouth.
Effects on Health Responsible for
symptoms of palpitation,
headache, dizziness, muscle
tightness, nausea, feeling of
weakness in the forearms, pains
in the neck, and other,
migraine-like symptoms in some
people. This substance is
recommended to be excluded
from the diets of hyperactive
children; it is also taboo in or
on food intended for babies and
young children.

**E340(a) Potassium
Dihydrogen Orthophosphate**
An emulsifying salt used as a
firming agent, to enhance the
antioxidant action of other
substances and maintain
acidity/alkalinity at a
determined level.
Effects on Health No known
health risks.

**E471 Mono- and Di-
glycerides of Fatty Acids**
Used to emulsify and stabilise.
Effects on Health Not known as a
health risk.

**E472(b) Lactic Acid Esters of
Mono- and Di-glycerides of
Fatty Acids** Used to emulsify,
stabilise, and as a texture
modifier.
Effects on Health No known
health risks.

E102 Tartrazine Gives yellow colouring to product.
Effects on Health Has been implicated with causing sleeplessness at night in hyperactive and food-sensitive children. Symptoms including skin rashes, hay fever, problems with breathing, blurred vision and purple skin patches are reported in susceptible people, particularly those who are aspirin sensitive or asthmatic.

E124 Ponceau 4R Gives red colouring to product.
Effects on Health One of the azo-dye family which is recommended to be excluded from the diets of hyperactive children. Adults who are aspirin sensitive or asthmatic may be affected.

E150 Caramel Gives brown colouring to product and is used as a flavouring.
Effects on Health A question mark as to its safety hangs over this additive. There has been a reduction in the number of kinds available to the food industry. Work is in hand to discover the safest form. One kind is produced with ammonia and has been shown to cause vitamin B6 deficiency in rats.

BATCHELORS CUP-O-SOUP

Sugar***   *Salt***

Modified Starch Used as thickener. An umbrella term for 18 substances not defined by 'E' numbers.
Effects on Health No suggestion that they are harmful.

621 Monosodium Glutamate Enhances the flavour of foods containing protein by stimulating the taste buds or increasing the degree of saliva produced in the mouth.
Effects on Health Responsible for symptoms of palpitation, headache, dizziness, muscle tightness, nausea, feeling of weakness in the forearms, pains in the neck, and other, migraine-like symptoms in some people. This substance is recommended to be excluded from the diets of hyperactive children; it is also taboo in or on food intended for babies and young children.

296 Malic Acid Gives flavouring; an acid derived from apples.
Effects on Health No known health risk.

E102 Tartrazine Gives yellow colouring to product.
Effects on Health Has been implicated with causing sleeplessness at night in hyperactive and food-sensitive children. Symptoms including

skin rashes, hay fever, problems with breathing, blurred vision and purple skin patches are reported in susceptible people, particularly those who are aspirin sensitive or asthmatic.

E124 Ponceau 4R Gives red colouring to product.
Effects on Health One of the azo-dye family which is recommended to be excluded from the diets of hyperactive children. Adults who are aspirin sensitive or asthmatic may be affected.

E320 Butylated Hydroxyanisole As an antioxidant this works alone or in conjunction with a synergist, i.e. citric acid or phosphoric acid, which enhances its effect. It prevents rancidity and also delays flavour deterioration due to oxidation.
Effects on Health It raises the lipid and cholesterol levels in the blood. Because it encourages the formation of metabolising enzymes in the liver there is the increased risk of the breakdown of important substances in the body such as vitamin D. The Hyperactive Children's Support Group recommend that this is not included in the diet of food-sensitive children. It is not permitted in foods intended for babies or young children, with the exception of its use to preserve added vitamin A.

E321 Butylated Hydroxytoluene Used as an antioxidant for food fats and oils.
Effects on Health Those who are sensitive to this antioxidant may develop rashes. It can increase the rate of breakdown of other substances in the body because of the developing of metabolising enzymes. Other reports link this additive with a possibility of reproductive failures, blood cell changes and effects on behaviour. The Hyperactive Children's Support Group include this on the list of substances not recommended for food-sensitive children; it is also taboo in foods intended for babies and young children with the exception of its use to preserve added vitamin A. There have been conflicting research reports on rats.

GATEWAY TOMATO SOUP MIX

Starch Used as thickener. An umbrella term for 18 substances not defined by 'E' numbers.
Effects on Health No suggestion that they are harmful.

621 Monosodium Glutamate Enhances the flavour of foods containing protein by stimulating the taste buds or increasing the degree of saliva produced in the mouth.
Effects on Health Responsible for

symptoms of palpitation, headache, dizziness, muscle tightness, nausea, feeling of weakness in the forearms, pains in the neck, and other, migraine-like symptoms in some people. This substance is recommended to be excluded from the diets of hyperactive children; it is also taboo in or on food intended for babies and young children.

Flavouring
Effects on Health Debatable, as no information is available. Many substances in this category are artificially synthesised; safety cannot be assumed.

296 Malic Acid Gives
flavouring; an acid derived from apples.
Effects on Health No known health risk.

E450(c) Sodium Polyphosphates Emulsifying
salts used to stabilise.
Effects on Health French research suggests that polyphosphates might block a number of enzymes, causing digestive disturbances.

E450(b) Pentasodium Triphosphate Used to provide
texture and as an emulsifying salt.
Effects on Health French research suggests that polyphosphates can block a number of enzymes causing digestive disturbances.

E450(a) Tetrasodium Diphosphate Maintains
acidity/alkalinity at a determined level; an emulsifying salt and stabiliser, also gelling agent.
Effects on Health No health risks known.

E339(b) Disodium Hydrogen Orthophosphate Balances
acidity/alkalinity at a determined level, stabilises, and is a gelling agent.
Effects on Health There are no known health risks.

E102 Tartrazine Gives yellow
colouring to product.
Effects on Health Has been implicated with causing sleeplessness at night in hyperactive and food-sensitive children. Symptoms including skin rashes, hay fever, problems with breathing, blurred vision and purple skin patches are reported in susceptible people, particularly those who are aspirin sensitive or asthmatic.

E124 Ponceau 4R Gives red
colouring to product.
Effects on Health One of the azo-dye family which is recommended to be excluded from the diets of hyperactive children. Adults who are aspirin sensitive or asthmatic may be affected.

See Note p. v

Peanut Butter

WHOLE EARTH
Sugar   *Salt***

No additives.

SAFEWAY SMOOTH PEANUT BUTTER

SUNPAT
Sugar**   *Salt***

WAITROSE
Sugar**   *Salt***

No additives.

also

SAINSBURY'S SMOOTH PEANUT BUTTER

E471 Mono- and Di-Glycerides of Fatty Acids Emulsifier and stabiliser.
Effects on Health No known health risk.

also

CO-OP PEANUT BUTTER

Pizzas from the Frozen Cabinet

HANDBAKED DE LUXE AMERICAN PIZZA (DELAWARE PIZZA BAKERY)
Sugar   *Salt***

No additives.

WAITROSE PIZZA MARINARA
Sugar**   *Salt***

Modified Starch Used as thickener. An umbrella term for 18 substances not defined by 'E' numbers.
Effects on Health No suggestion that they are harmful.

E415 Xanthan Gum Used to emulsify, stabilise or thicken.
Effects on Health There are no known health risks.

E250 Sodium Nitrite Preserves food and inhibits the growth of bacterium responsible for botulism.
Effects on Health Nitrites may interact with amines from foods in the stomach to form nitrosamines which are known to cause cancer in animals. They are also taboo in foods for babies and young children. Such an additive can cause allergic reactions and is on the list of foods not recommended by the Hyperactive Children's Support Group for children who are food sensitive.

also

KATIE'S KITCHEN PIZZA

TOWN CROWN PAN BAKE PIZZA

FINDUS FRENCH BREAD PIZZA
Sugar***   *Salt****

Modified Starch Used as thickener. An umbrella term for 18 substances not defined by 'E' numbers.
Effects on Health No suggestion that they are harmful.

E472(e) Mono- and Diacetyltartaric Acid Esters of Mono- and Di-glycerides of Fatty Acids Used to emulsify and stabilise.
Effects on Health There are no known health risks.

E450(c) Sodium Polyphosphates A stabiliser and emulsifying salt.
Effects on Health French research suggests that polyphosphates can cause the blockage of some enzymes and therefore digestive disturbances.

E301 Sodium L-ascorbate Provides vitamin C and is used as an antioxidant and to preserve colour.
Effects on Health There is no health risk unless usual dose is exceeded.

E250 Sodium Nitrite Preserves food and inhibits the growth of bacterium responsible for botulism.
Effects on Health Nitrites may interact with amines from foods in the stomach to form nitrosamines which are known to cause cancer in animals. They are also taboo in foods for babies and young children. Such an additive can cause allergic reactions and is on the list of those not recommended by the Hyperactive Children's Support Group.

E415 Xanthan Gum Used to emulsify, stabilise or thicken.
Effects on Health There are no known health risks though refined gums can cause stomach upsets if consumed in quantity.

Pork Pies from the Frozen Cabinet

PLUMTREE PORK PIES

*Sugar*** *Salt***

E450(b) Pentasodium Triphosphate Used to provide texture and is an emulsifying salt.
Effects on Health French research suggests that polyphosphates can block a number of enzymes, causing digestive disturbances.

E221 Sodium Sulphite A preservative and antioxidant in alkaline preparations.
Effects on Health Risk of danger to asthmatics as with all sulphites.

E301 Sodium L-ascorbate Provides vitamin C and is used as an antidioxidant and to preserve colour.
Effects on Health There is no health risk unless usual dose is exceeded.

TESCO NOTTINGHAMSHIRE PORK PIES

Sugar *Salt***

E321 Butylated Hydroxytoluene Used as an antioxidant for food fats and oils.
Effects on Health Those who are sensitive to this antioxidant may develop rashes. It can increase the rate of breakdown of other substances in the body, such as vitamin D, because of the developing of metabolising enzymes. Other reports link this additive with a possibility of reproductive failures, blood cell changes and effects on behaviour. The Hyperactive Children's Support Group include this on the list of substances not recommended for food-sensitive children. It is taboo in foods intended for babies and young children, with the exception of its use to preserve added vitamin A. There have been conflicting research reports on rats.

Starch Used as thickener. An umbrella term for 18 substances not defined by 'E' numbers.
Effects on Health No suggestion that they are harmful.

621 Monosodium Glutamate
Enhances the flavour of foods containing protein by stimulating the taste buds or increasing the degree of saliva produced in the mouth.
Effects on Health Responsible for symptoms of palpitation, headache, dizziness, muscle tightness, nausea, feeling of weakness in the forearms, pains in the neck, and other, migraine-like symptoms in some people. This substance is recommended by the Hyperactive Children's Support Group to be excluded from the diets of hyperactive children; it is also taboo in or on food intended for babies and young children.

WALL'S TRADITIONAL PORK PIES

Sugar   Salt**

E250 Sodium Nitrite Preserves food and inhibits the growth of bacterium responsible for botulism.
Effects on Health Nitrites may interact with amines from foods in the stomach to form nitrosamines which are known to cause cancer in animals. They are also taboo in foods for babies and young children. Such an additive can cause allergic reactions and is on the list of foods not recommended by the Hyperactive Children's Support Group.

E407 Carrageenan Used to thicken, emulsify or as a gelling agent.
Effects on Health It has been reported as a possible cause of ulcerative colitis and when degraded may be carcinogenic.

E301 Sodium L-ascorbate
Provides vitamin C and is used as an antioxidant and to preserve colour.
Effects on Health There is no health risk unless usual dose is exceeded.

E304 6-0-Palmitoyl-L-ascorbic Acid Used to preserve colour and as an antioxidant.
Effects on Health There is no known health risk.

E307 Synthetic Alpha-tocopherol Acts as an antioxidant and provides vitamin E.
Effects on Health There are no known health risks.

E450(c) Sodium Polyphosphates A stabiliser and emulsifying salt.
Effects on Health French research suggests that polyphosphates can cause the blockage of some enzymes and therefore digestive disturbances.

621 Monosodium Glutamate
Enhances the flavour of foods containing protein by stimulating the taste buds or increasing the degree of saliva produced in the mouth.
Effects on Health Responsible for symptoms of palpitation, headache, dizziness, muscle

tightness, nausea, feeling of weakness in the forearms, pains in the neck, and other, migraine-like symptoms in some people. This substance is recommended by the Hyperactive Children's Support Group to be excluded from the diets of hyperactive children; it is also taboo in or on food intended for babies and young children.

FINE FARE PORK PIES
Sugar**   *Salt***

E250 Sodium Nitrite Preserves food and inhibits the growth of bacterium responsible for botulism.
Effects on Health Nitrites may interact with amines from foods in the stomach to form nitrosamines which are known to cause cancer in animals. They are also taboo in foods for babies and young children. Such an additive can cause allergic reactions and is on the list of foods not recommended by the Hyperactive Children's Support Group for children who are food sensitive.

E450(a) Tetrasodium Diphosphate Maintains acidity/alkalinity at a determined level; an emulsifying salt and stabiliser, also gelling agent.

Effects on Health Not known as a health risk.

621 Monosodium Glutamate
Enhances the flavour of foods containing protein by stimulating the taste buds or increasing the degree of saliva produced in the mouth.
Effects on Health Responsible for symptoms of palpitation, headache, dizziness, muscle tightness, nausea, feeling of weakness in the forearms, pains in the neck, and other, migraine-like symptoms in some people. This substance is recommended by the Hyperactive Children's Support Group to be excluded from the diets of hyperactive children; it is also taboo in or on food intended for babies and young children.

E102 Tartrazine Gives yellow colouring to product.
Effects on Health Has been implicated with causing sleeplessness at night in hyperactive and food-sensitive children. Symptoms including skin rashes, hay fever, problems with breathing, blurred vision and purple skin patches are reported in susceptible people, particularly those who are aspirin sensitive or asthmatic.

E110 Sunset Yellow FCF
Gives yellow colouring to product.
Effects on Health One of the azo-dye family which is recommended to be excluded from the diets of hyperactive children. Adults may have an

allergic reaction with symptoms of skin rash, swollen blood vessels and gastric problems, especially if aspirin sensitive.

E124 Ponceau 4R Gives red colouring to product.
Effects on Health One of the azo-dye family which is recommended to be excluded from the diets of hyperactive children. Adults who are aspirin sensitive or asthmatic may be affected.

E128 Red 2G Gives red colouring to product.
Effects on Health Another synthetic dye which is recommended by the Hyperactive Children's Support Group to be excluded from the diets of food-sensitive children. There is a need for further studies into the safety of this colour.

Pork Sausages

WALKER'S PORK SAUSAGES
*Sugar   Salt***

621 Monosodium Glutamate Enhances the flavour of foods containing protein by stimulating the taste buds or increasing the degree of saliva produced in the mouth.
Effects on Health Responsible for symptoms of palpitation, headache, dizziness, muscle tightness, nausea, feeling of weakness in the forearms, pains in the neck, and other, migraine-like symptoms in some people. This substance is recommended to be excluded from the diets of hyperactive children; it is also taboo in or on food intended for babies and young children.

E450(a) Tetrasodium Diphosphate Maintains acidity/alkalinity at a determined level; an emulsifying salt and stabiliser, also gelling agent.
Effects on Health No health risks known.

E223 Sodium Metabisulphite Used as an antioxidant and to preserve.
Effects on Health A member of the sulphite family which is harmful to asthmatics. May cause gastric irritation because of the freeing of sulphurous acid. Can cause food allergies and aversions.

E307 Synthetic Alpha-tocopherol An antioxidant and supplies vitamin E.
Effects on Health No known health risk.

E304 6-0-Palmitoyl L-ascorbic Acid Preserves colour and is an antioxidant.
Effects on Health No health risk known.

WALL'S LINCOLNSHIRE PORK SAUSAGES

*Sugar   Salt***

Modified Starch Used as thickener. An umbrella term for 18 substances not defined by 'E' numbers.
Effects on Health No suggestion that they are harmful.

E450(b) Pentasodium Triphosphate or **Pentapotassium Triphosphate** Used to provide texture and to emulsify.
Effects on Health French research suggests that polyphosphates can block a number of enzymes, causing digestive disturbances.

E221 Sodium Sulphite Used to preserve; it is antimicrobial.
Effects on Health Asthmatics should beware as they are likely to have adverse reactions from all sulphites.

E128 Red 2G Colours food red.
Effects on Health There is need for further research into the effects of this additive. It is on the list of additives that are recommended by the

Hyperactive Children's Support Group to be excluded from the diets of hyperactive children.

BOWYERS LOW FAT PORK SAUSAGES

*Sugar***   *Salt***

E450(c) Sodium Polyphosphates Emulsifying salt which stabilises.
Effects on Health French research suggests that polyphosphates can block a number of enzymes, causing digestive disturbances.

E223 Sodium Metabisulphite Used as an antioxidant and to preserve.
Effects on Health A member of the sulphite family which is harmful to asthmatics. May cause gastric irritation because of the freeing of sulphurous acid. Can cause allergies and aversions.

621 Monosodium Glutamate Enhances the flavour of foods containing protein by stimulating the taste buds or increasing the degree of saliva produced in the mouth.
Effects on Health Responsible for symptoms of palpitation, headache, dizziness, muscle tightness, nausea, feeling of weakness in the forearms, pains in the neck, and other, migraine-like symptoms in some people. This substance is

recommended to be excluded from the diets of hyperactive children; it is also taboo in or on food intended for babies and young children.

E301 Sodium L-ascorbate
Preserves colour, is an antioxidant, provides vitamin C.
Effects on Health No risk to health.

E331 Sodium Citrates Acts as a synergist, i.e. enhances the effects of other antioxidants, and an emulsifying salt and controls the acid/alkaline level.
Effects on Health No known health risks.

E128 Red 2G Colours food red.
Effects on Health There is need for further research into the effects of this additive. It is on the list of azo-dyes that are recommended by the Hyperactive Children's Support Group to be excluded from the diets of hyperactive children.

TESCO PORK SAUSAGES WITH GARLIC
*Sugar   Salt***

Modified Starch Used as thickener. An umbrella term for 18 substances not defined by 'E' numbers.
Effects on Health No suggestion that they are harmful.

Flavouring
Effects on Health Debatable, as no information is available. Many substances in this category are artificially synthesised; safety cannot be assumed.

E450(c) Sodium Polyphosphates Emulsifying salt which stabilises.
Effects on Health French research suggests that polyphosphates can block a number of enzymes, causing digestive disturbances.

E270 Lactic Acid Used to preserve and also increases the antioxidant effect of other substances. Flavours product.
Effects on Health Very young or premature babies may have trouble metabolising lactic acid. No health risks known for adults.

E412 Guar Gum Thickener or dietary bulker.
Effects on Health Harmless except in excess when stomach cramps, nausea and flatulence might result.

E223 Sodium Metabisulphite Used as an antioxidant and to preserve.
Effects on Health A member of the sulphite family which is harmful to asthmatics. May cause gastric irritation by releasing sulphurous acid. Can cause food allergies and aversions.

E330 Citric Acid Stabilises the acidity of food substances, prevents discoloration of fruit,

keeps the flavour 'true' and retains vitamin C.
Effects on Health Needs to be consumed in very large quantities to erode teeth or irritate locally.

E128 Red 2G Colours food red.
Effects on Health There is need for further research into the effects of this additive. It is on the list of azo-dyes that are recommended by the Hyperactive Children's Support Group to be excluded from the diets of hyperactive children.

Potato Crisps

WAITROSE
Sugar   *Salt***

No additives.

also

SAFEWAY

SAINSBURY'S
Sugar   *Salt***

Flavourings
Effects on Health Debatable, as no information is available. Many substances in this category are artificially synthesised; safety cannot be assumed.

CO-OP
Sugar   *Salt***

E320 Butylated Hydroxyanisole As an antioxidant this works alone or in conjunction with a synergist, i.e. citric acid or phosphoric acid, which enhances its effect. It prevents rancidity and also delays flavour deterioration due to oxidation.
Effects on Health It raises the lipid and cholesterol levels in the blood. Because it encourages the formation of metabolising enzymes in the liver there is the increased risk of the breakdown of important substances in the body such as vitamin D. The Hyperactive Children's Support Group recommend that this is not included in the diet of food-sensitive children. It is not permitted in foods intended for babies or young children, with the exception of its use to preserve added vitamin A.

E321 Butylated Hydroxytoluene Used as an antioxidant for food fats and oils.

Effects on Health Those who are sensitive to this antioxidant may develop rashes. It can cause the breakdown of other substances in the body, such as vitamin D, because of the developing of metabolising enzymes. Other reports link this additive with a possibility of reproductive failures, blood cell changes and effects on behaviour. The Hyperactive Children's Support Group include this on the list of substances not recommended for food-sensitive children. It is taboo in foods intended for babies and young children, with the exception of its use to preserve added vitamin A. There have been conflicting research reports on rats.

also

KP

SMITH'S
Sugar   Salt**

E320 Butylated Hydroxyanisole
As an antioxidant this works alone or in conjunction with a synergist, i.e. citric acid or phosphoric acid, which enhances its effect. It prevents rancidity and also delays flavour deterioration due to oxidation.
Effects on Health It raises the lipid and cholesterol levels in the blood. Because it encourages the formation of metabolising enzymes in the liver there is the increased risk of the breakdown of important substances in the body such as vitamin D. The Hyperactive Children's Support Group recommend that this is not included in the diet of food-sensitive children. It is not permitted in foods intended for babies or young children, with the exception of its use to preserve added vitamin A.

E321 Butylated Hydroxytoluene
Used as an antioxidant for food fats and oils.
Effects on Health Those who are sensitive to this antioxidant may develop rashes. It can cause the breakdown of other substances in the body, such as vitamin D, because of the developing of metabolising enzymes. Other reports link this additive with a possibility of reproductive failures, blood cell changes and effects on behaviour. The Hyperactive Children's Support Group include this on the list of substances not recommended for food-sensitive children. It is taboo in foods intended for babies and young children, with the exception of its use to preserve added vitamin A. There have been conflicting research reports on rats.

E262 Sodium Hydrogen Diacetate
Used to preserve, and to inhibit microbes, particularly two forms which are heat resistant.
Effects on Health No health risks known.

621 Monosodium Glutamate
Enhances the flavour of foods
containing protein by
stimulating the taste buds or
increasing the degree of saliva
produced in the mouth.
Effects on Health Responsible for
symptoms of palpitation,
headache, dizziness, muscle
tightness, nausea, feeling of
weakness in the forearms, pains
in the neck, and other,
migraine-like symptoms in some
people. This substance is
recommended to be excluded
from the diets of hyperactive
children; it is also taboo in or
on food intended for babies and
young children.

**E635 Sodium 5'-
Ribonucleotide** Enhances
flavour.
Effects on Health Taboo in food
specially prepared for babies
and young children. People who
suffer from gout and related
conditions which demand
avoiding purines should not take
this substance. It is
recommended by the
Hyperactive Children's Support
Group to be excluded from the
diets of food-sensitive children.

Processed Cheese Slices

KRAFT SINGLES
Sugar   Salt**

E331 Sodium Citrates Acts as
a synergist, i.e. enhances the
effects of other antioxidants, and
as an emulsifying salt, and
controls the acid/alkaline level.
Effects on Health Not known as a
health risk.

**E339 Sodium Dihydrogen
Orthophosphate** Used to
enhance the effects of other
antioxidants, as a texture
improver and to balance
acidity/alkalinity at a
determined level.
Effects on Health Not known as a
health risk.

E202 Potassium Sorbate A
preservative that is antifungal
and antibacterial.
Effects on Health Not known as a
health risk.

SAINSBURY'S
PROCESSED CHEESE
SLICES
Sugar   Salt**

E331 Sodium Citrates Acts as
a synergist, i.e. enhances the
effects of other antioxidants, and
as an emulsifying salt, and
controls the acid/alkaline level.

Effects on Health No known health risks.

E200 Sorbic Acid Used to preserve and to inhibit the growth of moulds and yeasts.
Effects on Health There is a possibility of irritation to the skin.

E160 this could be **160(c) Capsanthin** Gives orangy colour.
Effects on Health No health risks known.
or
E160(b) Annatto Bixin Norbixin.
Effects on Health Safe except for reports of hives in some people.

Plus (for Co-op):
E450(c) Sodium Polyphosphates Emulsifying salt used to stabilise.
Effects on Health French research suggests that polyphosphates can block a number of enzymes, causing digestive disturbances.

also

CO-OP PROCESSED CHEESE SLICES

SAFEWAY PROCESSED CHEESE SLICES
Sugar   Salt**

E331 Sodium Citrates Acts as a synergist, i.e. enhances the effects of other antioxidants, and as an emulsifying salt, and controls the acid/alkaline level.
Effects on Health No known health risks.

E339 Sodium Dihydrogen Orthophosphates Used to enhance the effects of other antioxidants, as a texture improver and to balance acidity/alkalinity at a determined level.
Effects on Health No known health risks.

E450(c) Sodium Polyphosphates Emulsifying salt used to stabilise.
Effects on Health French research suggests that polyphosphates can block a number of enzymes, causing digestive disturbances.

E200 Sorbic Acid Used to preserve and to inhibit the growth of moulds and yeasts.
Effects on Health There is a possibility of irritation to the skin.

E160(a) Alpha-carotene, Beta-carotene, Gamma-carotene Gives a yellow-orange colour; converts to vitamin A in the body.
Effects on Health No known health risks.

E160(e) Beta-Apo-8'-Carotenal Gives an orange to reddish colouring.
Effects on Health No known health risk.

KERRYGOLD PROCESSED CHEESE SLICES

Sugar   Salt**

E339(c) Trisodium Orthophosphate An emulsifying salt; enhances the effects of other antioxidants and maintains acidity/alkalinity at a determined level.
Effects on Health No known health risks.

E450(a) Tetrasodium Diphosphate Maintains acidity/alkalinity at a determined level; an emulsifying salt and stabiliser, also gelling agent.

Effects on Health No health risks known.

E450(c) Sodium Polyphosphates Emulsifying salt, used to stabilise.
Effects on Health French research suggests that polyphosphates can block a number of enzymes thus causing digestive disturbances.

E202 Potassium Sorbate A preservative that is antifungal and antibacterial.
Effects on Health No known health risks.

E160(b) Annatto Bixin Norbixin Gives yellow to peach colour to product.
Effects on Health Safe except for reports of hives in some people.

Sage and Onion Stuffing

CHILTERN HERBS

Free from all artificial colouring, flavouring and preservatives.

CO-OP

Sugar   Salt**

Free from all artificial colouring, flavouring and preservatives.

also

FINE FARE

SAINSBURY'S

PAXO

SAFEWAY

WAITROSE

Sugar   Salt**

Natural flavouring.

KNORR

No added sugar or salt.

E320 Butylated Hydroxyanisole As an antioxidant this works alone or in conjunction with a synergist, i.e. citric acid or phosphoric acid, which enhances its effect. It prevents rancidity and also delays flavour deterioration due to oxidation.
Effects on Health It raises the lipid and cholesterol levels in the blood. Because it encourages the formation of metabolising enzymes in the liver there is the increased risk of the breakdown of important substances in the body such as vitamin D. The Hyperactive Children's Support Group recommend that this is not included in the diet of food-sensitive children. It is not permitted in foods intended for babies or young children, with the exception of its use to preserve added vitamin A.

Flavourings
Effects on Health Debatable, as no information is available. Many substances in this category are artificially synthesised; safety cannot be assumed.

621 Monosodium Glutamate Enhances the flavour of foods containing protein by stimulating the taste buds or increasing the degree of saliva produced in the mouth.
Effects on Health Responsible for symptoms of palpitation, headache, dizziness, muscle tightness, nausea, feeling of weakness in the forearms, pains in the neck, and other, migraine-like symptoms in some people. This substance is recommended to be excluded from the diets of hyperactive children; it is also taboo in or on food intended for babies and young children.

Salad Cream

HEINZ SALAD CREAM
Sugar**   *Salt***

Modified Starch Used as thickener. An umbrella term for 18 substances not defined by 'E' numbers.

Effects on Health No suggestion that they are harmful.

'Stabilisers' yet to be verified, but possibly **E405 Propane-1, 2-Diol Alginate, E410 Locust Bean Gum, E415 Corn Sugar Gum**
Effects on Health No known ill effects.

SAINSBURY'S SALAD CREAM

Sugar**   *Salt***

E410 Locust Bean Gum Used to stabilise or emulsify and also as a gelling agent.
Effects on Health No known ill effects.

E260 Acetic Acid Anti-bacterial; stabilises the acidity of food and dilutes colouring matter.
Effects on Health No known ill effects.

E102 Tartrazine Gives yellow colouring to food.
Effects on Health One of the azo-dye family which is recommended to be excluded from the diets of hyperactive children. Adults may have allergic reaction with symptoms of skin rash, swollen blood vessels and gastric problems, especially if aspirin sensitive.

also

TESCO SALAD CREAM

WAITROSE SALAD CREAM

Sugar**   *Salt***

E405 Propane-1, 2-Diol Alginate Used to stabilise or emulsify and thicken, and to disperse a substance in dilution or suspension.

Effects on Health There are no known health risks.

E415 Corn Sugar Gum Used to stabilise, emulsify and thicken.
Effects on Health There are no health risks known.

B413 Tragacanth Used to emulsify, stabilise and thicken.
Effects on Health Negligible, although when tragacanth is used on the skin contact dermatitis has been reported.

E102 Tartrazine Gives yellow colouring to food.
Effects on Health One of the azo-dye family which is recommended to be excluded from the diets of hyperactive children. Adults may have an allergic reaction with symptoms of skin rash, swollen blood vessels and gastric problems, especially if aspirin sensitive.

also

SAFEWAY

FINE FARE

CROSSE & BLACKWELL WAISTLINE

Sugar***   *Salt***

Modified Starch Used as thickener. An umbrella term for

18 substances not defined by 'E' numbers.
Effects on Health No suggestion that they are harmful.

'Emulsifier' possibly **E405 Propane-1, 2-Diol Alginate, E410 Locust Bean Gum, E415 Corn Sugar Gum.**
Effects on Health No known ill effects.

'Colour' possibly **E102 Tartrazine** Gives yellow colouring to food.
Effects on Health One of the azo-dye family which is recommended to be excluded from the diets of hyperactive children. Adults may have an allergic reaction with symptoms of skin rash, swollen blood vessels and gastric problems, especially if aspirin sensitive.

Savoury Rice

CROSSE & BLACKWELL'S 'RICE AND THINGS'
Sugar**   Salt**

621 Monosodium Glutamate Enhances the flavour of foods containing protein by stimulating the taste buds or increasing the degree of saliva produced in the mouth.
Effects on Health Responsible for symptoms of palpitation, headache, dizziness, muscle tightness, nausea, feeling of weakness in the forearms, pains in the neck, and other, migraine-like symptoms in some people. This substance is recommended to be excluded from the diets of hyperactive children; it is also taboo in or on food intended for babies and young children.

SAINSBURY'S SAVOURY RICE
Sugar**   Salt**

E330 Citric Acid Stabilises the acidity of food substances, prevents discoloration of fruit, keeps the flavour 'true' and retains vitamin C.
Effects on Health Needs to be consumed in very large quantities to erode teeth or irritate locally.

296 Malic Acid Gives flavouring; an acid derived from apples.
Effects on Health No known health risk.

551 Silicon Dioxide Prevents particles sticking together; thickens and emulsifies; used in suspensions and emulsions.
Effects on Health No known health risks.

Modified Starch Used as thickener. An umbrella term for 18 substances not defined by 'E' numbers.
Effects on Health No suggestion that they are harmful.

E102 Tartrazine Gives yellow colouring to product.
Effects on Health Has been implicated with causing sleeplessness at night in hyperactive and food-sensitive children. Symptoms including skin rashes, hay fever, problems with breathing, blurred vision and purple skin patches are reported in susceptible people, particularly those who are aspirin sensitive or asthmatic.

E124 Ponceau 4R Gives red colouring to product.
Effects on Health One of the azo-dye family which is recommended to be excluded from the diets of hyperactive children. Adults who are aspirin sensitive or asthmatic may be affected.

CO-OP SAVOURY RICE
Sugar*   *Salt**

621 Monosodium Glutamate Enhances the flavour of foods containing protein by stimulating the taste buds or increasing the degree of saliva produced in the mouth.

Effects on Health Responsible for symptoms of palpitation, headache, dizziness, muscle tightness, nausea, feeling of weakness in the forearms, pains in the neck, and other, migraine-like symptoms in some people. This substance is recommended to be excluded from the diets of hyperactive children; it is also taboo in or on food intended for babies and young children.

E320 Butylated Hydroxyanisole As an antioxidant this works alone or in conjunction with a synergist, i.e. citric acid or phosphoric acid, which enhances its effect. It prevents rancidity and also delays flavour deterioration due to oxidation.
Effects on Health It raises the lipid and cholesterol levels in the blood. Because it encourages the formation of metabolising enzymes in the liver there is the increased risk of the breakdown of important substances in the body such as vitamin D. The Hyperactive Children's Support Group recommend that this is not included in the diet of food-sensitive children. It is not permitted in foods intended for babies or young children, with the exception of its use to preserve added vitamin A.

E321 Butylated Hydroxytoluene Used as an antioxidant for food fats and oils.
Effects on Health Those who are sensitive to this antioxidant may

develop rashes. It can cause the breakdown of other substances in the body, such as vitamin D, because of the developing of metabolising enzymes. Other reports link this additive with a possibility of reproductive failures, blood cell changes and effects on behaviour. The Hyperactive Children's Support Group include this on the list of substances not recommended for food-sensitive children. It is taboo in foods intended for babies and young children, with the exception of its use to preserve added vitamin A. There have been conflicting research reports on rats.

E150 Caramel Gives brown colour to product and is used as a flavouring.
Effects on Health A question mark as to its safety hangs over this additive. There has been a reduction in the number of kinds available to the food industry. Work is in hand to discover the safest form. One kind is produced with ammonia and has been shown to cause vitamin B6 deficiency in rats.

BATCHELORS SAVOURY RICE
*Sugar   Salt***

E330 Citric Acid Stabilises the acidity of food substances, prevents discoloration of fruit, keeps the flavour 'true' and retains vitamin C.
Effects on Health Needs to be consumed in very large quantities to erode teeth or irritate locally.

296 Malic Acid Gives flavouring; an acid derived from apples.
Effects on Health No known health risk.

E124 Ponceau 4R Gives red colouring to product.
Effects on Health One of the azo-dye family which is recommended to be excluded from the diets of hyperactive children. Adults who are aspirin sensitive or asthmatic may be affected.

E220 Sulphur Dioxide Preserves and acts as an antioxidant or improving agent; stabilises vitamin C.
Effects on Health Irritates the alimentary canal; destroys much of flour's Vitamin E content. It is one of the additives which the Hyperactive Children's Support Group recommend be avoided by those who are food sensitive.

E320 Butylated Hydroxyanisole As an antioxidant this works alone or

in conjunction with a synergist, i.e. citric acid or phosphoric acid, which enhances its effect. It prevents rancidity and also delays flavour deterioration due to oxidation.
Effects on Health It raises the lipid and cholesterol levels in the blood. Because it encourages the formation of metabolising enzymes in the liver there is the increased risk of the breakdown of important substances in the body such as vitamin D. The Hyperactive Children's Support Group recommend that this is not included in the diet of food-sensitive children. It is not permitted in foods intended for babies or young children, with the exception of its use to preserve added vitamin A.

E321 Butylated Hydroxytoluene Used as an antioxidant for food fats and oils.
Effects on Health Those who are sensitive to this antioxidant may develop rashes. It can cause the breakdown of other substances in the body, such as vitamin D, because of the developing of metabolising enzymes. Other reports link this additive with a possibility of reproductive failures, blood cell changes and effects on behaviour. The Hyperactive Children's Support Group include this on the list of substances not recommended for food-sensitive children. It is taboo in foods intended for babies and young children, with the exception of its use to preserve added vitamin A. There have been conflicting research reports on rats.

Spaghetti in Tomato Sauce

SAINSBURY'S
Sugar**   *Salt***

Modified Starch Used as thickener. An umbrella term for 18 substances not defined by 'E' numbers.
Effects on Health No suggestion that they are harmful.

WAITROSE
Sugar**   *Salt***

Modified Starch Used as thickener. An umbrella term for 18 substances not defined by 'E' numbers.
Effects on Health No suggestion that they are harmful.

E330 Citric Acid Stabilises the acidity of food substances, prevents discoloration of fruit,

keeps the flavour 'true' and retains vitamin C.
Effects on Health Needs to be consumed in very large quantities to erode teeth or irritate locally.

also

CO-OP
Sugar***   *Salt***

HEINZ
Sugar**   *Salt***

Modified Starch Used as thickener. An umbrella term for 18 substances not defined by 'E' numbers.
Effects on Health No suggestion that they are harmful.

E330 Citric Acid Stabilises the acidity of food substances,

prevents discoloration of fruit, keeps the flavour 'true' and retains vitamin C.
Effects on Health Needs to be consumed in very large quantities to erode teeth or irritate locally.

621 Monosodium Glutamate
Enhances the flavour of foods containing protein by stimulating the taste buds or increasing the degree of saliva produced in the mouth.
Effects on Health Responsible for symptoms of palpitation, headache, dizziness, muscle tightness, nausea, feeling of weakness in the forearms, pains in the neck, and other, migraine-like symptoms in some people. This substance is recommended to be excluded from the diets of hyperactive children; it is also taboo in or on food intended for babies and young children.

also

SAFEWAY

Sparkling Lemonade

SPARKLING CORONA
Sugar***plus   *Salt*

E330 Citric Acid Stabilises the acidity of food substances, prevents discoloration of fruit, keeps the flavour 'true' and retains vitamin C.

Effects on Health Needs to be consumed in very large quantities to erode teeth or irritate locally.

Flavourings
Effects on Health Debatable, as no information is available. Many substances in this category are artificially

synthesised; safety cannot be
assumed.

E211 Sodium Benzoate
Preserves; is antibacterial and
antifungal.
Effects on Health People who are
prone to skin rashes or are
asthmatic may react with
allergic symptoms. This additive
is one that is recommended by
the Hyperactive Children's
Support Group to be avoided
by food-sensitive children and
adults who are aspirin sensitive.

also

SAINSBURY'S LEMONADE
Sugar***   *Salt*

CO-OP
Sugar***   *Salt*

SAFEWAY
Sugar*   *Salt*

Steak and Kidney Pies and Puddings in Tins

FRAY BENTOS STEAK AND KIDNEY PIE
Sugar   *Salt***

**E160(b) Annatto Bixin
Norbixin** Gives a peach to
yellow colour to product.
Effects on Health Safe except for
reports of hives in some people.

E100 Curcumin Gives an
orange-yellow tint to entire
product or surface only.
Effects on Health No known
health risks.

E150 Caramel Gives brown
colouring to product and is used
as a flavouring.
Effects on Health A question
mark as to its safety hangs over

this additive. There has been a
reduction in the number of
kinds available to the food
industry. Work is in hand to
discover the safest form. One
kind is produced with ammonia
and has been shown to cause
vitamin B6 deficiency in rats.

CO-OP STEAK AND KIDNEY PUDDING
Sugar   *Salt***

Modified Starch Used as
thickener. An umbrella term for
18 substances not defined by 'E'
numbers.

Effects on Health No suggestion that they are harmful.

621 Monosodium Glutamate

Enhances the flavour of foods containing protein by stimulating the taste buds or increasing the degree of saliva produced in the mouth.

Effects on Health Responsible for symptoms of palpitation, headache, dizziness, muscle tightness, nausea, feeling of weakness in the forearms, pains in the neck, and other, migraine-like symptoms in some people. This substance is recommended to be excluded from the diets of hyperactive children; it is also taboo in or on food intended for babies and young children.

E150 Caramel Gives brown colouring to product and is used as a flavouring.

Effects on Health A question mark as to its safety hangs over this additive. There has been a reduction in the number of kinds available to the food industry. Work is in hand to discover the safest form. One kind is produced with ammonia and has been shown to cause vitamin B6 deficiency in rats.

also

WALL'S STEAK AND KIDNEY PIE

SUTHERLANDS STEAK AND KIDNEY PIE

Strawberry Jam

JAMES ROBERTSON'S PURE FRUIT SPREAD

No added sugar.

E440(a) Pectin Gelling agent.
Effects on Health Not known as a health risk. Quantities in excess could cause distension and flatulence.

HARTLEY'S PURE FRUIT JAM

Sugar***   *Salt*

E440(a) Pectin Gelling Agent.
Effects on Health Not known as a health risk. Quantities in excess could cause distension and flatulence.

E330 Citric Acid Stabilises the acidity of food substances, prevents discoloration of fruit,

keeps the flavour 'true' and
retains vitamin C.
Effects on Health Needs to be
consumed in very large
quantities to erode teeth or
irritate locally.

163 Anthocyanins Natural
food colouring.
Effects on Health No harmful
effects known.

E331 Sodium Citrates
Enhances the effect of the citric
acid in product.
Effects on Health No harmful
effects known.

SAINSBURY'S STANDARD JAM
Sugar***   *Salt*

E440(a) Pectin Gelling Agent.
Effects on Health Not known as a
health risk. Quantities in excess
could cause distension and
flatulence.

E330 Citric Acid Stabilises the
acidity of food substances,
prevents discoloration of fruit,
keeps the flavour 'true' and
retains vitamin C.
Effects on Health Needs to be
consumed in very large
quantities to erode teeth or
irritate locally.

E124 Ponceau 4R Gives red
colour to product.
Effects on Health One of the azo-
dye family which is
recommended to be excluded
from the diets of hyperactive
children. Adults who are aspirin
sensitive or asthmatic may be
affected.

CO-OP STANDARD JAM
Sugar***   *Salt*

E440(a) Pectin Gelling agent.
Effects on Health Not known as a
health risk. Quantities in excess
could cause distension and
flatulence.

E330 Citric Acid Stabilises the
acidity of food substances,
prevents discoloration of fruit,
keeps the flavour 'true' and
retains vitamin C.
Effects on Health Needs to be
consumed in very large
quantities to erode teeth or
irritate locally.

E110 Sunset Yellow FCF
Gives yellow colouring to
product.
Effects on Health One of the azo-
dye family which is
recommended to be excluded
from the diets of hyperactive
children. Adults may have an
allergic reaction with symptoms
of skin rash, swollen blood
vessels and gastric problems,

especially if they are aspirin sensitive.

E124 Ponceau 4R Gives red colouring to product.
Effects on Health One of the azo-

dye family which is recommended to be excluded from the diets of hyperactive children. Adults who are aspirin sensitive or asthmatic may be affected.

Supreme Dessert Whips, Angel Delight, Supreme Delight and Dessert Mixes

CO-OP SUPREME DELIGHT
Sugar***   *Salt*

Modified Starch Used as thickener. An umbrella term for 18 substances not defined by 'E' numbers.
Effects on Health No suggestion that they are harmful.

E339 Sodium Dihydrogen Orthophosphate Used to enhance effects of other antioxidants, as a texture improver and to balance acidity/alkalinity at a determined level.
Effects on Health No known health risks.

E450(a) Tetrasodium Diphosphate Maintains acidity/alkalinity at determined level. An emulsifying salt and stabiliser, also gelling agent.
Effects on Health No known health risks.

E472(a) Acetic Acid Esters of Mono- and Di-glycerides of Fatty Acids Used to emulsify, stabilise, as a texture modifier and a coating agent.
Effects on Health No known health risks.

E472(b) Lactic Acid Esters of Mono- and Di-glycerides of Fatty Acids Used to emulsify, stabilise and as a texture modifier.
Effects on Health No known health risks.

E102 Tartrazine Gives yellow colouring to product.
Effects on Health Has been implicated with causing sleeplessness at night in hyperactive and food-sensitive children. Symptoms including skin rashes, hay fever, problems with breathing, blurred vision

and purple skin patches are reported in susceptible people, particularly those who are aspirin sensitive or asthmatic.

E110 Sunset Yellow FCF

Gives yellow colouring to product.

Effects on Health One of the azo-dye family which is recommended to be excluded from the diets of hyperactive children. Adults may have an allergic reaction with symptoms of skin rash, swollen blood vessels and gastric problems, especially if aspirin sensitive.

BIRD'S ANGEL DELIGHT

Sugar**   Salt*

Modified Starch Used as thickener. An umbrella term for 18 substances not defined by 'E' numbers.

Effects on Health No suggestion that they are harmful.

E477 Propane-1, 2-Diol Esters of Fatty Acids Used to emulsify and stabilise.

Effects on Health No known health risks.

E322 Lecithin Acts as an emulsifier and stabiliser; it is also an antioxidant and gives additional thickness to fats.

Effects on Health There are no known health risks; in fact,

lecithin is used therapeutically to mobilise fats in the body and has also been experimented with in the treatment of senile dementia.

E339 Sodium Dihydrogen Orthophosphate Used to enhance effects of other antioxidants, as a texture improver and to balance acidity/alkalinity at a determined level.

Effects on Health No known health risks.

E450(a) Tetrasodium Diphosphate Maintains acidity/alkalinity at a determined level; an emulsifying salt and stabiliser, also gelling agent.

Effects on Health No known health risks.

Flavourings

Effects on Health Debatable, as no information is available. Many substances in this category are artificially synthesised; safety cannot be assumed.

E150 Caramel Gives brown colouring to product and is used as a flavouring.

Effects on Health A question mark as to its safety hangs over this additive. There has been a reduction in the number of kinds available to the food industry. Work is in hand to discover the safest form. One kind is produced with ammonia and has been shown to cause vitamin B6 deficiency in rats.

E102 Tartrazine Gives yellow colouring to product.
Effects on Health Has been implicated with causing sleeplessness at night in hyperactive and food-sensitive children. Symptoms including skin rashes, hay fever, problems with breathing, blurred vision and purple skin patches are reported in susceptible people, particularly those who are aspirin sensitive or asthmatic.

E122 Carmoisine Gives red colouring to product.
Effects on Health This has been listed by the Hyperactive Children's Support Group as unsuitable for children who are food sensitive. An azo-dye, it may produce adverse reactions in those people who have aspirin allergy or are asthmatic. Such reactions can include skin rashes or swelling.

E160(a) Alpha-carotene, Beta-carotene, Gamma-carotene Gives a yellow-orange colour to product, converts to vitamin A in the body.
Effects on Health No known health risks.

E320 Butylated Hydroxyanisole As an antioxidant this works alone or in conjunction with a synergist, i.e. citric acid or phosphoric acid, which enhances its effect. It prevents rancidity and also delays flavour deterioration due to oxidation.
Effects on Health It raises the lipid and cholesterol levels in the blood. Because it encourages the formation of metabolising enzymes in the liver there is the increased risk of the breakdown of important substances in the body such as vitamin D. The Hyperactive Children's Support Group recommend that this is not included in the diet of food-sensitive children. It is not permitted in foods intended for babies or young children, with the exception of its use to preserve added vitamin A.

also

SAINSBURY'S SUPREME DESSERT WHIP

Sugar***   *Salt**

TESCO SUPREME DELIGHT

Sugar***   *Salt**

WAITROSE DESSERT MIX

Sugar***   *Salt**

FINE FARE SUPREME DESSERT

Sugar***   *Salt**

SAFEWAY SUPREME DELIGHT

Sugar***   *Salt**

Sweetmeal and Wheatmeal Digestive Biscuits

CO-OP DIGESTIVE WHEATMEAL

Sugar**   *Salt***

No additives.

GATEWAY DIGESTIVE SWEETMEAL

Sugar**   *Salt**

500 Sodium Bicarbonate
Used to balance alkaline/acid levels and to aerate.
Effects on Health Not known as a health risk.

503 Ammonium Carbonate
Used to maintain the alkaline/acid pH at a determined level; to aerate.
Effects on Health Not known as a health risk.

Plus (for McVitie's)
E334 Tartaric Acid
Used as an antioxidant, either alone or as a synergist, i.e. to enhance the antioxidant effect of other substances.
Effects on Health No known health risk except as an irritant if taken in very large quantities.

also
McVITIE'S NATURAL CHOICE

Sugar***   *Salt**

SAFEWAY DIGESTIVE SWEETMEAL

Sugar***   *Salt***

E320 Butylated Hydroxyanisole
As an antioxidant this works alone or in conjunction with a synergist, i.e. citric acid or phosphoric acid, which enhances its effect. It prevents rancidity and also delays flavour deterioration due to oxidation.
Effects on Health It raises the lipid and cholesterol levels in the blood. Because it encourages the formation of metabolising enzymes in the liver there is the increased risk of the breakdown of important substances in the body such as vitamin D. The Hyperactive Children's Support Group recommend that this is not included in the diet of food-sensitive children. It is not permitted in foods intended for babies or young children, with the exception of its use to preserve added vitamin A.

Plus (for Tesco)
E472(e) Mono- and Diacetyltartaric Acid Esters of Mono- and Di-glycerides of Fatty Acids Used to emulsify or stabilise.
Effects on Health There are no known health risks.

also

SAINSBURY'S DIGESTIVE SWEETMEAL

TESCO SWEETMEAL

WAITROSE

Sugar*** *Salt***

500 Sodium Bicarbonate Used to balance alkaline/acid levels and to aerate.
Effects on Health Not known as a health risk.

503 Ammonium Carbonate
Used to maintain the alkaline/acid pH at a determined level; to aerate.
Effects on Health Not known as a health risk.

E320 Butylated Hydroxyanisole As an antioxidant this works alone or in conjunction with a synergist, i.e. citric acid or phosphoric acid, which enhances its effect. It prevents rancidity and also delays flavour deterioration due to oxidation.
Effects on Health It raises the lipid and cholesterol levels in the blood. Because it encourages the formation of metabolising enzymes in the liver there is the increased risk of the breakdown of important substances in the body such as vitamin D. The Hyperactive Children's Support Group recommend that this is not included in the diet of food-sensitive children. It is not permitted in foods intended for babies or young children, with the exception of its use to preserve added vitamin A.

Sweet Pickled Onions

KEY MARKETS
*Sugar*** *Salt***

260 Acetic Acid Antibacterial; used to stabilise the acidity of food and dilute colouring matter.
Effects on Health No known ill effects.

E150 Caramel Gives brown colour to product and is used as a flavouring.
Effects on Health A question mark as to its safety hangs over this additive. There has been a reduction in the number of kinds available to the food industry. Work is in hand to discover the safest form. One kind is produced with ammonia and has been shown to cause vitamin B6 deficiency in rats.

E223 Sodium Metabisulphite A preservative and antioxidant.
Effects on Health A member of the sulphite family which is harmful to asthmatics; may cause gastric irritation because of the liberation of sulphurous acid. Can cause allergies and food aversion.

also

CO-OP
*Sugar*** *Salt***

SAFEWAY
*Sugar**** *Salt***

HAYWARDS
*Sugar**** *Salt***

E150 Caramel Gives brown colour to product and is used as a flavouring.
Effects on Health A question mark as to its safety hangs over this additive. There has been a reduction in the number of kinds available to the food industry. Work is in hand to discover the safest form. One kind is produced with ammonia and has been shown to cause vitamin B6 deficiency in rats.

E200 Sorbic Acid A preservative which inhibits the growth of moulds and yeasts.
Effects on Health There is a possibility of skin irritation.

E223 Sodium Metabisulphite A preservative and antioxidant.
Effects on Health A member of the sulphite family which is harmful to asthmatics; may cause gastric irritation because of the liberation of sulphurous acid. Can cause allergies and food aversion.

Sweet Pickles

HEINZ PLOUGHMAN'S PICKLE

*Sugar*** *Salt***

Modified Starch Used as thickener. An umbrella term for 18 substances not defined by 'E' numbers.
Effects on Health No suggestion that they are harmful.

E260 Acetic Acid Antibacterial, used to stabilise the acidity of food and dilute colouring matter.
Effects on Health No known ill effects.

E150 Caramel Gives brown colour to product and is used as a flavouring.
Effects on Health A question mark as to its safety hangs over this additive. There has been a reduction in the number of kinds available to the food industry. Work is in hand to discover the safest form. One kind is produced with ammonia and has been shown to cause vitamin B6 deficiency in rats.

also

BRANSTON PICKLE

CO-OP'S SWEET PICKLE

TESCO SWEET PICKLE

SAINSBURY'S SWEET PICKLE

SAFEWAY SWEET PICKLE

PAN YAN ORIGINAL PICKLE

*Sugar**** *Salt***

Modified Starch Used as thickener. An umbrella term for 18 substances not defined by 'E' numbers.
Effects on Health No suggestion that they are harmful.

E150 Caramel Gives brown colour to product and is used as a flavouring.
Effects on Health A question mark as to its safety hangs over this additive. There has been a reduction in the number of kinds available to the food industry. Work is in hand to discover the safest form. One kind is produced with ammonia and has been shown to cause vitamin B6 deficiency in rats.

E155 Brown HT Gives brown colour to product.
Effects on Health As an azo-dye this should be avoided by children who are hyperactive or food sensitive. It may also cause adverse reactions in those who are aspirin sensitive, asthmatic or prone to allergy.

E102 Tartrazine Gives yellow colour to product.
Effects on Health It has been implicated with causing sleeplessness at night in hyperactive and food-sensitive children. Symptoms including skin rashes, hay fever, problems with breathing, blurred vision and purple skin patches are reported in susceptible people, particularly those who are aspirin sensitive.

Flavouring
Effects on Health Debatable, as no information is available. Many substances in this category are artificially synthesised; safety cannot be assumed.

E220 Sulphur Dioxide
Preserves and acts as an antioxidant or improving agent. Stabilises vitamin C.
Effects on Health Irritates the alimentary food canal; destroys much of flour's vitamin E content. It is one of the additives which the Hyperactive Children's Support Group recommend be avoided by those who are food sensitive.

Swiss Roll

WAITROSE SWISS ROLL
Sugar ***   *Salt* *

E471 Mono- and Di-glycerides of Fatty Acids An emulsifier and stabiliser.
Effects on Health No known health risks.

E470 Sodium Potassium and Calcium Salts of Fatty Acids An emulsifier and stabiliser which serves to prevent particles sticking together.
Effects on Health No known health risk.

E475 Polyglycerol Esters of Fatty Acids
Emulsifier and stabiliser.
Effects on Health No known health risk.

E420 Sorbitol Syrup Used for sweetening and also to prevent products from drying out.
Effects on Health When taken to excess it can cause flatulence and distension of stomach. It is, however, of use to diabetics as it does not raise the blood sugar level significantly and is well tolerated.

E102 Tartrazine Gives yellow colouring to food.

Effects on Health Has been implicated with causing sleeplessness at night in hyperactive and food-sensitive children. Symptoms including skin rashes, hay fever, problems with breathing, blurred vision and purple skin patches are reported in susceptible people, particularly those who are aspirin sensitive or asthmatic.

E110 Sunset Yellow FCF

Gives yellow colouring to food.
Effects on Health One of the azo-dye family which is recommended to be excluded from the diets of hyperactive children. Adults may have an allergic reaction with symptoms of skin rash, swollen blood vessels and gastric problems, especially if aspirin sensitive.

E160(a) Alpha-carotene, Beta-carotene, Gamma-carotene

Gives orange-yellow colour to product and converts to vitamin A in the body.
Effects on Health No known health risks.

Flavours

Effects on Health Debatable, as no information is available. Many substances in this category are artificially synthesised; safety cannot be assumed.

SAINSBURY'S SWISS ROLL

Sugar***   *Salt*

E330 Citric Acid Stabilises the

acidity of food substances, prevents discoloration of fruit, keeps the flavour 'true' and retains vitamin C.
Effects on Health Needs to be consumed in very large quantities to erode teeth or irritate locally.

E440(a) Pectin Gelling agent, emulsifier and stabiliser.
Effects on Health No known health risks.

E122 Carmoisine Gives red colouring to food.
Effects on Health This has been listed by the Hyperactive Children's Support Group as unsuitable for children who are food sensitive. An azo-dye, it may produce adverse reactions in people who have aspirin allergy or are asthmatic. Such reactions can include skin rashes or swelling.

E132 Indigo Carmine Gives blue colouring to food.
Effects on Health Another of the azo-dye family which should be avoided by anyone who has a tendency to allergy. Some of the allergic reactions that may be caused are skin rash, itching and breathing problems. It can also cause nausea, vomiting, high blood pressure and hypertension.

Starch Used as thickener. An umbrella term for 18 substances not defined by 'E' numbers.
Effects on Health No suggestion that they are harmful.

E470 Sodium Potassium and Calcium Salts of Fatty Acids

An emulsifier and stabiliser

which serves to prevent particles sticking together.
Effects on Health No known health risks.

E471 Mono- and Di-glycerides of Fatty Acids An emulsifier and stabiliser.
Effects on Health No known health risks.

E102 Tartrazine Gives yellow colouring to food.
Effects on Health Has been implicated with causing sleeplessness at night in hyperactive and food-sensitive children. Symptoms including skin rashes, hay fever, problems with breathing, blurred vision and purple skin patches are reported in susceptible people, particularly those who are aspirin sensitive or asthmatic.

E110 Sunset Yellow FCF Gives yellow colouring to food.
Effects on Health One of the azo-dye family which is recommended to be excluded from the diets of hyperactive children. Adults may have an allergic reaction with symptoms of skin rash, swollen blood vessels and gastric problems, especially if aspirin sensitive.

E202 Potassium Sorbate A preservative that is antifungal and antibacterial.
Effects on Health No known health risks.

MEMORY LANE SWISS ROLL

Sugar **   *Salt* *

E440(a) Liquid Pectin Emulsifier and gelling agent.
Effects on Health No adverse effects although large amounts could cause temporary stomach distension or flatulence.

Modified Starch Used as thickener. An umbrella term for 18 substances not defined by 'E' numbers.
Effects on Health No suggestion that they are harmful.

E465 Ethylmethylcellulose Used to emulsify, stabilise and as a foaming agent.
Effects on Health No known health risks.

E471 Mono- and Di-glycerides of Fatty Acids An emulsifier and stabiliser.
Effects on Health No known health risks.

E475 Polyglycerol Esters of Fatty Acids An emulsifier and stabiliser.
Effects on Health No known health risks.

E330 Citric Acid Stabilises the acidity of food substances, prevents discoloration of fruit, keeps the flavour 'true' and retains vitamin C.
Effects on Health Needs to be consumed in very large quantities to erode teeth or irritate locally.

E331 Sodium Citrates Acts as a synergist, i.e. enhances the

effects of other antioxidants; an
emulsifying salt and controls
acid/alkaline levels.
Effects on Health No known
health risks.

E102 Tartrazine Gives yellow
colouring to food.
Effects on Health Has been
implicated with causing
sleeplessness at night in
hyperactive and food-sensitive
children. Symptoms including
skin rashes, hay fever, problems
with breathing, blurred vision
and purple skin patches are
reported in susceptible people,
particularly those who are
aspirin sensitive or asthmatic.

E110 Sunset Yellow FCF
Gives yellow colouring to food.
Effects on Health One of the azo-
dye family which is
recommended to be excluded
from the diets of hyperactive
children. Adults may have an
allergic reaction with symptoms
of skin rash, swollen blood
vessels and gastric problems,
especially if aspirin sensitive.

E123 Amaranth A widely used
red colour agent.
Effects on Health An azo-dye, it
should be avoided by people
who are sensitive to aspirin as it
may cause a skin rash. The
Hyperactive Children's Support
Group recommend it is
excluded from the diets of food-
sensitive children.

E124 Ponceau 4R Gives red
colouring to food.
Effects on Health One of the azo-
dye family which is
recommended to be excluded
from the diets of hyperactive
children. Adults who are aspirin

sensitive or asthmatic may be
affected.

Flavouring
Effects on Health Debatable, as
no information is available.
Many substances in this
category are artificially
synthesised; safety cannot be
assumed.

E202 Potassium Sorbate A
preservative that is antifungal
and antibacterial.
Effects on Health No known
health risks.

E282 Calcium Propionate
Used to preserve and to inhibit
microbial moulds, especially two
which are heat resistant.
Effects on Health No known
health risks.

LYONS SWISS ROLL
Sugar***   Salt*

E420 Sorbitol Syrup Used for
sweetening and also to prevent
products from drying out.
Effects on Health When taken to
excess it can cause flatulence
and distension of stomach. It is,
however, of use to diabetics as it
does not raise the blood sugar
level significantly and is well
tolerated.

**E471 Mono- and Di-
glycerides of Fatty Acids** An
emulsifier and stabiliser.
Effects on Health No known
health risks.

Modified Starch Used as
thickener. An umbrella term for

18 substances not defined by 'E' numbers.
Effects on Health No suggestion that they are harmful.

Flavouring
Effects on Health Debatable, as no information is available. Many substances in this category are artificially synthesised; safety cannot be assumed.

E202 Potassium Sorbate A preservative that is antifungal and antibacterial.
Effects on Health No known health risks.

E102 Tartrazine Gives yellow colouring to food.
Effects on Health Has been implicated with causing sleeplessness at night in hyperactive and food-sensitive children. Symptoms including skin rashes, hay fever, problems with breathing, blurred vision and purple skin patches are reported in susceptible people, particularly those who are aspirin sensitive or asthmatic.

E110 Sunset Yellow FCF Gives yellow colouring to food.
Effects on Health One of the azo-dye family which is recommended to be excluded from the diets of hyperactive children. Adults may have an allergic reaction with symptoms of skin rash, swollen blood vessels and gastric problems, especially if aspirin sensitive.

E122 Carmoisine Gives red colouring to food.
Effects on Health This has been listed by the Hyperactive Children's Support Group as unsuitable for children who are food sensitive. An azo-dye, it may produce adverse reactions in people who have an aspirin allergy or are asthmatic. Such reactions can include skin rashes or swelling.

E124 Ponceau 4R Gives red colouring to food.
Effects on Health One of the azo-dye family which is recommended to be excluded from the diets of hyperactive children. Adults who are aspirin sensitive or asthmatic may be affected.

E127 Erythrosine Gives red colouring to food. A coal-tar dye.
Effects on Health This additive can cause sensitivity to light and has also been recommended by the Hyperactive Children's Support Group to be excluded from the diets of hyperactive children. Because it contains 577mg of iodine per gram, there is a risk that the consuming of a number of foods which contain E127 might cause an over-active thyroid.

E150 Caramel Gives brown colouring to product and is used as a flavouring.
Effects on Health A question mark as to its safety hangs over this additive. There has been a reduction in the number of kinds available to the food industry. Work is in hand to discover the safest form. One kind which is produced with ammonia has been shown to cause vitamin B6 deficiency in rats.

Table Jelly—Orange and Other Citrus Flavours

SAINSBURY'S TANGERINE FLAVOUR JELLY

Sugar***   *Salt*

E330 Citric Acid Stabilises the acidity of food substances, prevents discoloration of fruit, keeps the flavour 'true' and retains vitamin C.
Effects on Health Needs to be consumed in very large quantities to erode teeth or irritate locally.

E102 Tartrazine Gives yellow colouring to product.
Effects on Health Has been implicated with causing sleeplessness at night in hyperactive and food-sensitive children. Symptoms including skin rashes, hay fever, problems with breathing, blurred vision and purple skin patches are reported in susceptible people, particularly those who are aspirin sensitive or asthmatic.

E124 Ponceau 4R Gives red colouring to product.
Effects on Health One of the azo-dye family which is recommended to be excluded from the diets of hyperactive children. Adults who are aspirin sensitive or asthmatic may be affected.

Plus (for Safeway and Fine Fare):

Flavouring
Effects on Health Debatable, as no information is available. Many substances in this category are artificially synthesised; safety cannot be assumed.

Plus (for Fine Fare):
E260 Acetic Acid Antibacterial. Used to stabilise the acidity of food and dilute colouring matter.
Effects on Health No known ill effects.

also

SAFEWAY ORANGE FLAVOUR JELLY

FINE FARE YELLOW PACK ORANGE FLAVOUR JELLY

GATEWAY LEMON FLAVOUR JELLY

Sugar***   *Salt*

E330 Citric Acid Stabilises the acidity of food substances, prevents discoloration of fruit, keeps the flavour 'true' and retains vitamin C.
Effects on Health Needs to be

consumed in very large quantities to erode teeth or irritate locally.

E260 Acetic Acid
Antibacterial, used to stabilise the acidity of food and dilute colouring matter.
Effects on Health No known ill effects.

Flavouring
Effects on Health Debatable, as no information is available. Many substances in this category are artificially synthesised; safety cannot be assumed.

E331 Sodium Citrates
Acts as a synergist, i.e. enhances the effects of other antioxidants, and as an emulsifying salt, and controls acid/alkaline levels.
Effects on Health No known ill effects.

E102 Tartrazine
Gives yellow colouring to product.
Effects on Health Has been implicated with causing sleeplessness at night in hyperactive and food-sensitive children. Symptoms including skin rashes, hay fever, problems with breathing, blurred vision and purple skin patches are reported in susceptible people, particularly those who are aspirin sensitive or asthmatic.

E110 Sunset Yellow FCF
Gives yellow colouring to product.
Effects on Health One of the azo-dye family which is recommended to be excluded from the diets of hyperactive children. Adults may have an

allergic reaction with symptoms of skin rash, swollen blood vessels and gastric problems, especially if aspirin sensitive.

ROWNTREE'S TABLE JELLY ORANGE FLAVOUR

*Sugar ***plus   Salt*

E330 Citric Acid
Stabilises the acidity of food substances, prevents discoloration of fruit, keeps the flavour 'true' and retains vitamin C.
Effects on Health Needs to be consumed in very large quantities to erode teeth or irritate locally.

E331 Sodium Citrates
Acts as a synergist, i.e. enhances the effects of other antioxidants, and as an emulsifying salt, and controls acid/alkaline levels.
Effects on Health No known ill effects.

E260 Acetic Acid
Antibacterial, used to stabilise the acidity of food and dilute colouring matter.
Effects on Health No known ill effects.

Flavouring
Effects on Health Debatable, as no information is available. Many substances in this category are artificially synthesised; safety cannot be assumed.

E102 Tartrazine
Gives yellow colouring to product.

Effects on Health Has been implicated with causing sleeplessness at night in hyperactive and food-sensitive children. Symptoms including skin rashes, hay fever, problems with breathing, blurred vision and purple skin patches are reported in susceptible people, particularly those who are aspirin sensitive or asthmatic.

E122 Carmoisine Gives red colouring to product.
Effects on Health This has been listed by the Hyperactive Children's Support Group as unsuitable for children who are food sensitive. An azo-dye, it may produce adverse reactions in people who have aspirin allergy or are asthmatic. Such reactions can include skin rashes or swelling.

E127 Erythrosine Gives red colouring to product. A coal-tar dye.
Effects on Health This additive can cause sensitivity to light and has also been recommended by the Hyperactive Children's Support Group to be excluded from the diets of food-sensitive and hyperactive children. Because it contains some 577mg of iodine per gram, there is a risk that the consuming of a number of foods which contain E127 might cause an over-active thyroid.

Thousand Islands Dressing

SAFEWAY
Sugar**   *Salt***

Modified Starch Used as thickener. An umbrella term for 18 substances not defined by 'E' numbers.
Effects on Health No suggestion that they are harmful.

E202 Potassium Sorbate A preservative that is antifungal and antibacterial.
Effects on Health No known ill effects.

E410 Locust Bean Gum Used to stabilise and emulsify; also a gelling agent.
Effects on Health There are no known health risks. Pods of the bean have been consumed since Biblical times. Refined gums can cause stomach upsets if consumed in quantity.

E200 Sorbic Acid A preservative and inhibitor of yeast and mould growth.
Effects on Health Possibility of irritating skin.

also

TESCO

HEINZ
Sugar**   *Salt***

Modified Starch Used as thickener. An umbrella term for

18 substances not defined by 'E' numbers.
Effects on Health No suggestion that they are harmful.

E202 Potassium Sorbate A preservative which is antifungal and antibacterial.
Effects on Health No known ill effects.

E260 Acetic Acid
Antibacterial; used to stabilise the acidity of food and dilute colouring matter.
Effects on Health No known ill effects.

'Stabilisers' as yet unspecified. These could be **E405 Propane-1, 2-Diol Alginate** Used to stabilise or emulsify, to thicken, and to disperse a substance in solution or suspension.
Effects on Health No known ill effects.

E410 Locust Bean Gum Used to stabilise and emulsify; also a gelling agent.
Effects on Health There are no known health risks. Pods of the bean have been consumed since Biblical times. Refined gums eaten in quantity can cause stomach upsets.

E415 Corn Sugar Gum Used to stabilise, emulsify or thicken.
Effects on Health No known ill effects.

'Preservative' yet to be specified. Possibly **E202 Potassium Sorbate** A preservative which is antifungal and antibacterial.
Effects on Health No known ill effects.

KRAFT

Sugar***   *Salt****

E405 Propane-1, 2-Diol Alginate Used to stabilise or emulsify, to thicken, and to disperse a substance in solution or suspension.
Effects on Health No known ill effects.

Flavouring
Effects on Health Debatable, as no information is available. Many substances in this category are artificially synthesised; safety cannot be assumed.

BATCHELORS

Sugar***   *Salt***

Modified Starch Used as thickener. An umbrella term for 18 substances not defined by 'E' numbers.
Effects on Health No suggestion that they are harmful.

E160(c) Capsanthin Gives orange colour to product.
Effects on Health No known ill effects.

E160(a) Alpha-carotene, Beta-carotene, Gamma-carotene Gives an orange-yellow colour to product and converts to vitamin A in the body.
Effects on Health No known ill effects.

E150 Caramel Gives brown colour to product and is used as a flavouring.
Effects on Health A question mark as to its safety hangs over this additive. There has been a reduction in the number of kinds available to the food industry. Work is in hand to discover the safest form. One kind which is produced with ammonia has been shown to cause vitamin B6 deficiency in rats.

Flavourings
Effects on Health Debatable, as no information is available. Many substances in this category are artificially synthesised; safety cannot be assumed.

E200 Sorbic Acid Used to preserve and to inhibit growth of moulds and yeasts.
Effects on Health There is a possibility of irritation of skin.

E320 Butylated Hydroxyanisole As an antioxidant this works alone or in conjunction with a synergist, i.e. citric acid or phosphoric acid, which enhances its effect. It prevents rancidity and also delays flavour deterioration due to oxidation.
Effects on Health It raises the lipid and cholesterol levels in the blood. Because it encourages the formation of metabolising enzymes in the liver there is an increased risk of the breakdown of important substances in the body such as vitamin D. The Hyperactive Children's Support Group recommend that this substance is not included in the diet of food-sensitive children. It is not permitted in foods intended for babies and young children with the exception of its use to preserve added vitamin A.

Tinned Meat Stew

CO-OP STEWED STEAK IN GRAVY
Sugar   *Salt***

E150 Caramel Gives brown colour to product and is used as flavouring.
Effects on Health A question mark as to its safety hangs over this additive. There has been a reduction in the number of kinds available to the food industry. Work is in hand to discover the safest form. One kind which is produced with ammonia has been shown to cause vitamin B6 deficiency in rats.

FRAY BENTOS STEWED STEAK IN GRAVY

*Sugar   Salt***

Modified Starch Used as thickener. An umbrella term for 18 substances not defined by 'E' numbers.
Effects on Health No suggestion that they are harmful.

E150 Caramel Gives brown colour to product and is used as flavouring.
Effects on Health A question mark as to its safety hangs over this additive. There has been a reduction in the number of kinds available to the food industry. Work is in hand to discover the safest form. One kind which is produced with ammonia has been shown to cause vitamin B6 deficiency in rats.

SAINSBURY'S IRISH STEW

*Sugar   Salt***

Modified Starch and **Starch** Used as thickeners. An umbrella term for 18 substances not defined by 'E' numbers.
Effects on Health No suggestion that they are harmful.

621 Monosodium Glutamate Enhances the flavour of foods

containing protein by stimulating the taste buds or increasing the degree of saliva produced in the mouth.
Effects on Health Responsible for symptoms of palpitation, headache, dizziness, nausea, muscle tightness, a feeling of weakness in the forearms, pains in the neck, and other, migraine-like symptoms in some people. This substance is recommended to be excluded from the diets of hyperactive children; it is also taboo in or on foods intended for babies and young children.

E412 Guar Gum Used to thicken; a bulking agent.
Effects on Health Harmless except when consumed to excess when nausea, flatulence and stomach cramps might occur.

E410 Locust Bean Gum Used to stabilise and emulsify; a gelling agent.
Effects on Health There are no known health risks. Pods of the bean have been consumed since Biblical times, but refined guns can cause stomach upsets if consumed in quantity.

PRINCES STEWED STEAK IN GRAVY

*Sugar   Salt***

621 Monosodium Glutamate Enhances the flavour of foods containing protein by stimulating the taste buds or increasing the degree of saliva produced in the mouth.

Effects on Health Responsible for symptoms of palpitation, headache, dizziness, nausea, muscle tightness, a feeling of weakness in the forearms, pains in the neck, and other, migraine-like symptoms in some people. This substance is recommended to be excluded from the diets of hyperactive children; it is also taboo in or on foods intended for babies and young children.

E150 Caramel Gives brown colour to product and is used as flavouring.

Effects on Health A question mark as to its safety hangs over this additive. There has been a reduction in the number of kinds available to the food industry. Work is in hand to discover the safest form. One kind which is produced with ammonia has been shown to cause vitamin B6 deficiency in rats.

Tinned Peas

WAITROSE PETIT POIS

Sugar**   *Salt***

No added colouring or flavouring.

CO-OP MARROWFAT PROCESSED PEAS

Sugar**   *Salt***

E102 Tartrazine Gives yellow colouring to product.

Effects on Health Has been implicated with causing sleeplessness at night in hyperactive and food-sensitive children. Symptoms including skin rashes, hay fever, problems with breathing, blurred vision and purple skin patches are reported in susceptible people, particularly those who are aspirin sensitive or asthmatic.

E142 Acid Brilliant Green Gives green colouring to product.

Effects on Health No ill effects are reported although as a synthetic dye it might affect hypersensitive children and those who suffer from asthma or are aspirin sensitive.

Flavouring

Effects on Health Debatable, as no information is available. Many substances in this category are artificially synthesised; safety cannot be assumed.

also

SMEDLEY'S GARDEN PEAS

SAFEWAY GARDEN PEAS

MORTON GARDEN PEAS

WAITROSE SMALL PROCESSED PEAS

BATCHELORS MUSHY PEAS

Sugar **   *Salt* **

E133 Brilliant Blue FCF
Provides a dark blue colouring which can convert to green when combined with tartrazine.
Effects on Health As an azo-dye it is a substance that has been recommended to be excluded from the diet of hyperactive children.

E102 Tartrazine Gives yellow colouring to product.
Effects on Health One of the azo-dye family which is recommended to be excluded from the diets of hyperactive children. Adults may have an allergic reaction with symptoms of skin rash, swollen blood vessels and gastric problems, especially if aspirin sensitive.

FARROWS GIANT MARROWFAT

Sugar **   *Salt* **

E133 Brilliant Blue FCF
Provides a dark blue colouring which can convert to green when combined with tartrazine.
Effects on Health As an azo-dye it is a substance that has been recommended to be excluded from the diet of hyperactive children.

E102 Tartrazine Gives yellow colouring to product.
Effects on Health One of the azo-dye family which is recommended to be excluded from the diets of hyperactive children. Adults may have an allergic reaction with symptoms of skin rash, swollen blood vessels and gastric problems, especially if aspirin sensitive.

Flavouring
Effects on Health Debatable, as no information is available. Many substances in this category are artificially synthesised; safety cannot be assumed.

Tinned Pork Luncheon Meat

SAINSBURY'S

Sugar   *Salt***

Modified Starch Used as thickener. An umbrella term for 18 substances not defined by 'E' numbers.
Effects on Health No suggestion that they are harmful.

E450(b) Pentasodium Triphosphate Used to provide texture and is an emulsifying salt.
Effects on Health French research suggests that polyphosphates can block a number of enzymes, causing digestive disturbances.

621 Monosodium Glutamate Enhances the flavour of foods containing protein by stimulating the taste buds or increasing the degree of saliva produced in the mouth.
Effects on Health Responsible for symptoms of palpitation, headache, dizziness, nausea, muscle tightness, a feeling of weakness in the forearms, pains in the neck, and other, migraine-like symptoms in some people. This substance is recommended to be excluded from the diets of hyperactive children; it is also taboo in or on foods intended for babies and young children.

E250 Sodium Nitrite Preserves food and inhibits the growth of bacterium responsible for botulism.
Effects on Health Nitrites may interact with amines from foods in the stomach to form nitrosamines which are known to cause cancer in animals. They are taboo in foods for babies and young children. Such an additive can cause allergic reactions and is on the list of substances not recommended by the Hyperactive Children's Support Group.

E127 Erythrosine Gives red colouring to food. An azo-dye.
Effects on Health This additive can cause sensitivity to light and has also been recommended by the Hyperactive Children's Support Group to be excluded from the diets of hyperactive children. Because it contains 577mg of iodine per gram, there is a risk that the consuming of a number of foods which contain E127 might cause an over-active thyroid.

PRINCES
Sugar **   *Salt* **

Modified Starch Used as thickener. An umbrella term for 18 substances not defined by 'E' numbers.
Effects on Health No suggestion that they are harmful.

E450(c) Sodium Polyphosphates Emulsifying salts used to stabilise.
Effects on Health French research suggests that polyphosphates might block a number of enzymes, causing digestive disturbances.

621 Monosodium Glutamate Enhances the flavour of foods containing protein by stimulating the taste buds or increasing the degree of saliva produced in the mouth.
Effects on Health Responsible for symptoms of palpitation, headache, dizziness, nausea, muscle tightness, a feeling of weakness in the forearms, pains in the neck, and other, migraine-like symptoms in some people. This substance is recommended to be excluded from the diets of hyperactive children. It is also taboo in or on foods intended for babies and young children.

E301 Sodium L-ascorbate Provides vitamin C and is used as an antioxidant and to preserve colour.
Effects on Health There is no health risk unless usual dose is exceeded.

E127 Erythrosine Gives red colouring to food. An azo-dye.
Effects on Health This additive can cause sensitivity to light and has also been recommended by the Hyperactive Children's Support Group to be excluded from the diets of hyperactive children. Because it contains 577mg of iodine per gram there is a risk that the consuming of a number of foods which contain E127 might cause an over-active thyroid.

E250 Sodium Nitrite Preserves food and inhibits the growth of bacterium responsible for botulism.
Effects on Health Nitrites may interact with amines from foods in the stomach to form nitrosamines which are known to cause cancer in animals. They are taboo in foods for babies and young children. Such an additive can cause allergic reactions and is on the list of substances not recommended by the Hyperactive Children's Support Group.

also

TESCO VALUE LTD

FINE FARE YELLOW PACK
Sugar   *Salt* **

CO-OP DANISH PORK LUNCHEON PORK MEAT

Sugar ** *Salt* **

Modified Starch Used as thickener. An umbrella term for 18 substances not defined by 'E' numbers.
Effects on Health No suggestion that they are harmful.

E339 Sodium Dihydrogen Orthophosphate Used to enhance effects of other antioxidants, as a texture improver and to balance acidity/alkalinity at a determined level.
Effects on Health No known health risks.

E450(a) Tetrasodium Diphosphate Maintains acidity/alkalinity at a determined level; an emulsifying salt and stabiliser, also gelling agent.
Effects on Health No known health risks.

E450(b) Pentasodium Triphosphate Used to provide texture and is an emulsifying salt.
Effects on Health French research suggests that polyphosphates can block a number of enzymes, causing digestive disturbances.

E450(c) Sodium Polyphosphates Emulsifying salts used to stabilise.
Effects on Health French research suggests that polyphosphates might block a number of enzymes, causing digestive disturbances.

E250 Sodium Nitrite Preserves food and inhibits the growth of bacterium responsible for botulism.
Effects on Health Nitrites may interact with amines from foods in the stomach to form nitrosamines which are known to cause cancer in animals. They are taboo in foods for babies and young children. Such an additive can cause allergic reactions and is on the list of substances not recommended by the Hyperactive Children's Support Group.

Yoghurt (Strawberry)

ST IVEL REAL

No added sugar, free from artificial colourings and preservatives.

CHAMBOURCY

Sugar ** *Salt*

No added starch, colour, preservative or artificial flavouring.

SAINSBURY'S STRAWBERRY
Sugar **   *Salt*

Modified Starch Used as thickener. An umbrella term for 18 substances not defined by 'E' numbers.
Effects on Health No suggestion that they are harmful.

E330 Citric Acid Stabilises the acidity of food substances, prevents discoloration of fruit, keeps the flavour 'true' and retains vitamin C.
Effects on Health Needs to be consumed in very large quantities to erode teeth or irritate locally.

E124 Ponceau 4R Gives red colouring to product.
Effects on Health One of the azo-dye family which is recommended to be excluded from the diets of hyperactive children. Adults who are aspirin sensitive or asthmatic may be affected.

Plus (for Safeway, Waitrose, Tesco and Munch Bunch):

Flavourings
Effects on Health Debatable, as no information is available. Many substances in this category are artificially synthesised; safety cannot be assumed.

also
SAFEWAY

WAITROSE
Sugar *

TESCO

MUNCH BUNCH

TESCO RICH STRAWBERRY
Sugar **

E124 Ponceau 4R Gives red colouring to product.
Effects on Health One of the azo-dye family which is recommended to be excluded from the diets of hyperactive children. Adults who are aspirin sensitive or asthmatic may be affected.

E122 Carmoisine Gives red colouring to food.
Effects on Health This has been listed by the Hyperactive Children's Support Group as unsuitable for children who are food sensitive. An azo-dye, it may produce adverse reactions in people who have an aspirin allergy or are asthmatic. Such reactions can include skin rashes or swelling.

Modified Starch Used as thickener. An umbrella term for 18 substances not defined by 'E' numbers.
Effects on Health No suggestion that they are harmful.

E330 Citric Acid Stabilises the acidity of food substances, prevents discoloration of fruit, keeps the flavour 'true' and retains vitamin C.
Effects on Health Needs to be consumed in very large quantities to erode teeth or irritate locally.

E412 Guar Gum Used to thicken; a bulking agent.

Effects on Health Harmless except when consumed to excess when nausea, flatulence and stomach cramps might occur.

Flavourings
Effects on Health Debatable, as no information is available. Many substances in this category are artificially synthesised; safety cannot be assumed.

Cracking the Code: A Complete System

(Reproduced by kind permission of the Soil Association)

Colourings

BEWARE		SUSPECT	SAFE	
AZO DYES				
E100			E100 Turmeric	E100
E101			E101 Vitamin B2	E101
E102	E102 Tartrazine			E102
E104	E104 Quinoline Yellow			E104
107	107 Yellow 2G			107
E110	E110 Sunset Yellow			E110
E120	E120 Cochineal[3]			E120
E122	E122 Carmoisine, Azorubine			E122
E123	E123 Amaranth			E123
E124	E124 Ponceau 4R			E124
E127	E127 Erythrosine			E127
128	128 Red 2G			128
E131	E131 Patent Blue V			E131
E132	E132 Indigo Carmine			E132
133	133 Brilliant Blue			133
E140			E140 } Chlorophyll	E140
E141			E141 }	E141
E142	E142 Green S, Lissamine Green			E142
E150		E150 Caramel[2]		E150
E151	E151 Black PN			E151
E153			E153 Carbon	E153
154	154 Brown FK			154
155	155 Brown HT			155
E160			E160 } Relatives of	E160
E161			E161 } Vitamin E	E161
E162			E162 }	E162
E163			E163 Anthocyanins	E163
E170			E170 Chalk	E170
E171			E171 Titanium Oxide	E171
E172			E172 Iron Oxides	E172
E173		E173 Aluminium		E173
E174		E174 Silver		E174
E175		E175 Gold		E175
E180	E180 Pigment Rubine			E180

Notes

(1)	**Azo Dyes**	Dangerous to asthmatics, hyperactive children, those sensitive to aspirin.
(2)	**Caramel**	Prepared by various processes, some of which may incur vitamin B6 deficiency. The definition is being simplified. 98% by weight of all the colouring used in foods.
(3)	**Cochineal**	Can cause hyperactivity in children.

Preservatives

BEWARE		SUSPECT	SAFE	
E200			E200 ⎫	E200
E201			E201 ⎪	E201
E202			E202 ⎬ Sorbates[1]	E202
E203			E203 ⎭	E203
E210	E210 ⎫			E210
E211	E211 ⎪			E211
E212	E212 ⎬ Benzoates[2]			E212
E213	E213 ⎪			E213
E214	E214 ⎭			E214
E215	E215			E215
E216	E216 ⎫			E216
E217	E217 ⎬ Complex Benzoates[2]			E217
E218	E218 ⎪			E218
E219	E219 ⎭			E219
E220	E220 ⎫			E220
E221	E221 ⎪			E221
E222	E222 ⎪			E222
E223	E223 ⎬ Sulphites, Sulphur Dioxide[3]			E223
E224	E224 ⎪			E224
E226	E226 ⎪			E226
E227	E227 ⎭			E227
E230	E230 ⎫			E230
E231	E231 ⎬ Biphenyls[4]			E231
E232	E232 ⎭			E232
E233			E233 ⎫ On citrus and	E233
E234			E234 ⎭ banana skins	E234
E236		E236 ⎫		E236
E237		E237 ⎬ Formates[21]		E237
E238		E238 ⎭		E238
E239	E239 Hexamine[9]			E239
E249	E249 ⎫			E249
E250	E250 ⎬ Nitrites[8]			E250
E251	E251 ⎭			E251
E252	E252 Nitrate[8]			E252
E260			E260 ⎫	E260
E261			E261 ⎪ Acetates	E261
E262			E262 ⎬ (Vinegar)	E262
E263			E263 ⎭	E263
E270		E270 Lactic Acid[5]		E270
E280			E280 ⎫	E280
E281			E281 ⎪ Propionates[6]	E281
E282			E282 ⎬	E282
E283			E283 ⎭	E283
E290		E290 Carbon Dioxide[7]		E290
E296			E296	E296
E297			E297	E297

Notes

1)	**E200-203 Sorbic Acid**	From mountain ash berries.
2)	**E210-219 Benzoates**	Dangerous to allergics, asthmatics, hypersensitives.
3)	**E220-227 Sulphur Dioxide** etc.	Beware on uncooked raw fruit. Dangerous to asthmatics, hypersensitives. Lowers Vitamin E content of flour. Lowers Vitamin B1 content of various foods.
4)	**E230-232 Biphenyls**	Beware on citrus peel. Some probably penetrates to the flesh.
5)	**E270 Lactic Acid**	Beware in food for very small babies.
6)	**E280-283 Propionates**	Migraine sufferers may do well to avoid these.
7)	**E290 Carbon Dioxide**	Enhances absorption in stomach. Increases effect of alcohol.

(8) **E249-252 Nitrite, Nitrate**	Highly controversial. May combine with amines in the stomach, producing highly cancer-forming nitrosamines. Interacts dangerously with the blood cells of infants.	
(9) **E239 Hexamine**	May upset intestines, urinary system, or less often the skin. Possibly cancer forming.	

Anti-Oxidants, Emulsifiers, Stabilisers, Miscellaneous

BEWARE	SUSPECT	SAFE	
E300		E300 ⎫	E300
E301		E301 ⎬ Ascorbates	E301
E302		E302 ⎬	E302
E304		E304 ⎭	E304
E306		E306 ⎫	E306
E307		E307 ⎬ Vitamin E	E307
E308		E308 ⎬	E308
E309		E309 ⎭	E309
E310	E310 ⎫		E310
E311	E311 ⎬ Gallates[1]		E311
E312	E312 ⎭		E312
E320	E320 BHA[22]		E320
E321	E321 BHT[22]		E321
E322		E322 Lecithins	E322
E325	E325 ⎫		E325
E326	E326 ⎬ Lactates[2]		E326
E327	E327 ⎭		E327
E330		E330 ⎫	E330
E331		E331 ⎬ Citrates	E331
E332		E332 ⎬	E332
E333		E333 ⎭	E333
E334		E334 ⎫	E334
E335		E335 ⎬	E335
E336		E336 ⎬ Tartrates	E336
E337		E337 ⎬	E337
E338		E338 ⎭	E338
E339		E339 ⎫	E339
E340		E340 ⎬ Phosphates	E340
E341		E341 ⎭	E341
350		350 ⎫	350
351		351 ⎬ Malates	351
352		352 ⎭	352
353		353 Metatartaric Acid	353
355		355 Adipic Acid	355
363		363 Succinic Acid	363
370	370 Heptonolactone		370
375		375 Vitamin B	375
380		380 ⎫ Citrates	380
381		381 ⎭	381
E385	E385 Salt of EDTA[3]		E385
E400		E400 ⎫	E400
E401		E401 ⎬	E401
E402		E402 ⎬ Alginates	E402
E403		E403 ⎬ (seaweed)	E403
E404		E404 ⎬	E404
E405		E405 ⎭	E405
E406		E406 Agar	E406
E407	E407 Carrageenan[4]		E407
E410		E410 ⎫	E410
E412		E412 ⎬ Natural Gums	E412
E413		E413 ⎭	E413

BEWARE	SUSPECT	SAFE
E414	E414 Acacia Gum[5]	E414
E415	E415 ⎱ Natural Gums	E415
E416	E416 ⎰	E416
E420		E420 Sorbitol
E421	E421 Mannitol[6]	E421
E422		E422 Glycerol
430 ⎱ Stearates[7]		430
431 ⎰		431
432	432 ⎱	432
433	433 ⎟	433
434	434 ⎬ Polyoxyethylenes[8]	434
435	435 ⎟	435
436	436 ⎰	436
E440		E440 Pectin
442	442 Ammonium phosphatides	442
E450 Polyphosphates[9]		E450
E460		E460 ⎱
E461		E461 ⎟
E463		E463 ⎬ Celluloses
E464		E464 ⎟
E465		E465 ⎟
E466		E466 ⎰
E470	E470 ⎱	E470
E471	E471 ⎟	E471
E472	E472 ⎬ Fats, soaps[20]	E472
E473	E473 ⎟	E473
E474	E474 ⎰	E474
E475	E475 ⎱	E475
E476	E476 ⎟	E476
E477	E477 ⎬ Fats, soaps[20]	E477
E478	E478 ⎰	E478
E481	E481 ⎱	E481
E482	E482 ⎬ Fatty Acids	E482
E483	E483 ⎰	E483
491	491 ⎱	491
492	492 ⎟	492
493	493 ⎬ Sorbitans	493
494	494 ⎟	494
495	495 ⎰	495
		500 ⎱
		501 ⎟
		502 ⎬ Carbonates
		503 ⎟
		504 ⎰
507	507 ⎱	507
508	508 ⎬ Chlorides[11]	508
509	509 ⎟	509
510	510 ⎰	510
513	513 Sulphuric Acid[12]	513
514	514 Sodium Sulphate	514
515		515 Potassium Sulphate
516		516 Calcium Sulphate
518		518 Magnesium Sulphate
524	524 Caustic Soda[12]	524
525	525 Caustic Potash[12]	525
526		526 Calcium Hydroxide
527	527 Ammonium Hydroxide[12]	527
528		528 Magnesium Hydroxide
529	529 Quick Lime	529
530	530 Magnesium Oxide	530
535 ⎱ Ferrocyanides[13]		535
536 ⎰		536
541 Phosphate[14]		541
542	542 Bone Phosphate[15]	542

BEWARE		SUSPECT	SAFE	
544	544 ⎫			54
545	545 ⎭ Polyphosphates[9]			54
551			551 ⎫	55
552			552 ⎭ Silicates	55
553			553 Talc	55
554	554 ⎫			55
556	556 ⎭ Silicates[14]			55
558		558 Bentonite		55
559			559 Kaolin	55
570			570 ⎫	57
572			572 ⎭ Stearate	57
575		575 Glucono delta Lactone		57
576			576 ⎫	57
577			577 ⎬ Gluconates	57
578			578 ⎭	57

FLAVOUR ENHANCERS

BEWARE		SUSPECT	SAFE	
620	620 Glutamic Acid			62
621	621 Monosodium Glutamate			62
622	622 ⎫			62
623	623 ⎭ Other Glutamates			62
627	627 Guanylate[17]			62
631	631 Inosinate[17]			63
635	635 Guanylate and Inosinate[17]			63
636	636 Maltol 'fresh bake' flavour[16]			63
637	637 Ethyl Maltol - sweetener[16]			63
900		900 Dimethicone		90
901			901 Bees Wax	90
903			903 Carnauba Wax	90
904			904 Shellac	90
905	905 Mineral Hydrocarbons[18]			90
907			907 Wax	90
920			920 Amino-acid derivative	92
924	924 Bromate[19]			92
925	925 Chlorine[19]			92
927	927 Azoformamide[20]			92

Notes

(1)	**Gallates**	A benzoate, not permitted in foods intended for young children. May harm asthmatics, those sensitive to aspirin, hyperactive children.
(2)	**Lactates**	To be avoided for very young children.
(3)	**EDTA**	May disrupt absorption of Iron, Zinc and Copper.
(4)	**Carrageenan**	Irish moss, a seaweed; may however cause ulcerative colitis, and may decompose to a carcinogen. Worst in drinks.
(5)	**Acacia Gum**	Known to be toxic at 100%; some confections get up to 45%!
(6)	**Mannitol**	Occasionally produces hypersensitivity.
(7)	**Stearates**	May produce skin allergies; a possible cause of kidney stones.
(8)	**Polyoxyethylenes**	Very little information available; may alter absorption of fat.
(9)	**Polyphosphates**	Used to retain moisture in meat products, they can easily be abused to inflate the weight (and price) of a product, though this is an offence in Britain. Beware particularly of chicken and ham
(10)	**Sorbitan esters**	Very little information available. May increase gut absorption of paraffins, which are irritant.
(11)	**Chlorides**	Several are capable of corrosive effects on the intestine, and perhaps disturbances of body fluids. Very little information available.
(12)	**Acids & Alkalis**	These are all corrosive, in sufficient quantity. Little information is available as to how they are used.
(13)	**Ferrocyanides**	We depend for our safety on nothing disturbing their low absorption from the intestine.

(14)	**Contains Aluminium**	Suspected to be capable of harm in some people.
(15)	**Bone phosphate**	Vegetarians would wish to avoid this.
(16)	**Flavour enhancers**	Make the food taste better than it really is. Along with salt and sugar, largely responsible for distorting appetites and encouraging over-eating. Almost certainly implicated in the epidemic of obesity in young people.
(17)	**Purines**	Prohibited from foods intended for young children. Gout sufferers, and rheumatics generally, should avoid these.
(18)	**Hydrocarbons**	That is liquid paraffins, which as cathartics may cause anal seepage, and stool looseness, in some people.
(19)	**Bleaches**	Doubts exist about safety. In flour, destroys Vitamin E and other nutrients. Capable of major intestinal upset, and convulsions.
(20)	**Fats, soaps**	Little information is given. Could in quantity interfere with intestinal function and absorption.
(21)	**Formates**	Formic acid very irritant to skin. All have diuretic effects (on the kidneys).
(22)	**BHA, BHT**	Currently subjects of intensive safety research, because of many doubts. Either may contribute indirectly to wastage of body stores of Vitamin D, or cause hyperactivity. Neither permitted in foods intended for young children.

Index of Foods

Index of Additives